The Hebrew Book of Revelation

"I Am the Aleph and the Tav"

English Translation

Miles R. Jones, Ph.D.

Preview Edition © Copyright 2024 Miles R. Jones
ISBN # 978-1-957488-09-7

"Yehovah gave the Word; Great was the company of those that published it!"
Psalm 68:11

Great Publishing Company
Benai Emunah Institute
Kerrville, Texas

Acknowledgements

Miles R. Jones, Chief Editor
Jonathan Felt, Associate Editor & Archivist
Pamela Lutzker, Associate Editor & Manager of Publications
Janice Baca, Senior Hebrew Editor
Patrick J. McGuire, Layout Design & Video Producer

—

MS Transcriptions: Caroline Shemesh, Deanna Amsler,
Stephanie Shiflet, Nigel Lloyd-Jones

—

MS Scholars and Committee Contributors for this Interlinear:
Alan Esselbach, aja-anon, Anna Knecht, Bryan Williams,
Caroline Shemesh, David Winer, Deanna Amsler, Diane
DeLeon, Janice Baca, Jennifer Webster, Jennifer Howell, John
Abel, Jonathan Felt, Jonathan Meyer, Kay Agnew, Kurt Sutton,
Kyle Gadd, Miles R. Jones, Naamah Hadi, Nick Strickland,
Matthew Chamberlain, Pam Lutzker, Rocky Webb, Sebastian
Rhinehart, Uwani Richardson

—

Other Active Contributors & Specialists world-wide as of
Aug 2023: Andreas Hurter (German), Anita Burke (h.t.),
Anita Jones (h.tr.), Anna Knecht (h.t.ldr), Arie Kralt (w.tr., MS
Research), Bel Guiste (h.t.), Bernardo Partida (Spanish), Bryan

Williams (training h.t.), Brooke Chabert (MS research), Carlos Comacho (Spanish), Caroline Shemesh (Hebrew), Christian Pope (h.tr.), Cindy Abel (h.tr.a), Dale Brunk (h.t.), Daisy Collins (h.t.), David Cocetti (h.t.), Deanna Amsler (h.t.), Dev Greenhill P.h.D (h.t.), Donna Beccia Carick P.h.D (mizmor), Donna King (h.t.), Drew Sartorius (webmaster), Elana Sauber (h.t.), Harry Taylor (mizmor), Eric Jessen (h.tr.a.), Horacio Nunez (Latin America Coordinator), Howard Johnston (h.t.), Hugo DeSJack Carruth (h.t.), Jacob Lansford (h.t.), Janet Flores (t.w.), Jeff Sciba (h.tr.), Jennifer Howell (h.tr.), Jennifer Webster (h.tr.ldr.), Jeremiah Mowen (h.t.), Jim Gordon (board of directors), Gordon Hays (h.t.), John Abel (h.tr.ldr), John Reed Austin (mizmor ldr), John Lansford (h.t.), Jonathan Meyers (h.t.), Joseph Collins (h.t.), Joshua Erickson Family (h.tr.a), Judy Busby (h.t.), Juli Ocean (t.w.), Julie Lansford (h.t.), Kim Shaffer Edie (h.tr.), Kurt Sutton (h.tr.a), Kyle Gadd (tech), Maria Hammerlein (office), Linda Nadal (h.t.), Lisa Schoenegge (h.tr.), Lisa-Mary Holsome (h.t.), Marie Gentry (h.tr.a.), Matthew Chamberlain (h.tr.ldr), Matthew Shaw (h.t.), Michael Chabert (MS Research), Michael Howell (h.t.), Michael Mallory (social media), Mike Blair (h.t.), Mrs. Catherine Jones (board), Naama Hadi (h.tr.), Nathan Swasey (h.t.), Nick Strickland (h.tr.), Nigel Lloyd-Jones (h.t.), Pam Laurion (h.tr.), Paul Pequegnat (Hebrew), Peggy Brunk (office), Phillip Bradshaw (mizmor), Rae Lloyd-Jones (h.t.), Rebekah Williams (h.tr.a), Revis Daggett (h.t.), Robert Bjerk (tr), Robert Mallard (office), Robert C Hendrix (h.tr.a), Rocky Webb (h.tr.), Tom Martincic (h.t.), Tommy Cole P.h.D (h.t), Stephanie Shiflet (h.t.), Sara Morgan (h.t.), Sebastian Rhinehart (h.tr.a.), Uwani Richardson (h.tr.a), Uzziel Herrera (Spanish), Yehoyakim Dürr (German)

—

(h.t.) Hebrew Transcriber, (h.t.ldr) Hebrew Transcriber Leader, (h.tr.) Hebrew Translator, (h.tr.ldr) Hebrew Translation Team Leader, (h.tr.a) Hebrew Translation Assistant, (mizmor) Psalmist and Musician, (h.t.a) Hebrew Translation Advisor, (t.w.) Technical Writer, (w.tr.) Waldensian Translator

Preface

Benai Emunah Institute

This project is an outgrowth of the amazing discovery in 2014 by Dr. Miles R. Jones of the oldest surviving Hebrew manuscript of the New Testament Gospels, Vatican ebr. 100, (called the Hebrew Gospels from Catalonia or HGC) found bound behind the tales of Sinbad in Hebrew. As he researched the provenance of this document, and began to translate it, Dr. Jones realized that the details in this document were quite different from those of the standard Bible of today which comes from the Greek.

He painstakingly documented these differences, drawing from quotations of the Early Church Fathers for authentication. When he cross-referenced them to the Hebrew Gospel of Matthew by George Howard (often referred to as the Shem Tov Hebrew Matthew), he found many agreements in the two texts that were not in the Greek text.

Dr. Jones decided that if there were two manuscripts with the Hebrew New Testament - when previously there was thought to be none - there must be more. Dr. Jones returned to Europe in 2019 to seek out more. He found them. Among those found are two copies of the entire New Testament found by Claudius Buchanan in Cochin, India in a "synagogue of the black Jews." These manuscripts became part of the Moses Gaster collection, which was added to the British Library.

The first manuscript, found at the Cambridge University Library, Cambridge, England, is the oldest copy and is a combination of MS Oo.1.32 and Oo.1.16.2 (bound together). It was supposedly translated or recopied by Ezekiel Rahabi, a chief merchant of the Dutch East India Company, using Sephardic script in the early 1700's. He was unable to finish the translation and hired Leopold van Dort, a converted Jew, to complete the project.

The second copy of the Hebrew New Testament is MS Gaster 1616 in the Rylands Library in Manchester, England. It came from the same place, Cochin, India and is a copy of the Rahabi manuscript, in modern square script, written by David Cohen, working with Van Dort. Since then, Dr. Jones and the Benai Emunah Institute have recovered more than fifty manuscripts of the Brit Hadashah (New Testament) in Hebrew from libraries all over the world. Of these we have five that are complete compilations of all the Gospels, books, and letters of the New Testament. Before Dr. Jones work - there were no known complete Hebrew manuscripts of Revelation. There was only the Hazon manuscript of the Sloane collection Ms. 273 translated by Nehemiah Gordon. It is the first chapter and a half, going only to Revelation 2:12.

Now we have various manuscripts including the Cambridge MS Oo.1.16.2, Gaster MS 1616, Freiberg MS HS-314, Paris MS 131 and the Hazon-Sloane MS 273. This is the first compilation ever of those Hebrew manuscripts of the Book of Revelation.

Cambridge Oo.1.16.2

Gaster 1616

Cochin Manuscripts

Here is the Interlinear Chart of Revelation 1:1 from Freiberg Hebrew Manuscript HS-314.

Revelation 1:1

Hebrew Text Translation: The Revelation of Yeshua the Messiah, which Elohim gave to him (John), to reveal to his servants the things that they must do in the time of the harvest.

King James Version (KJV): The Revelation of Jesus Christ, which God gave unto him, to shew unto his servants things which must shortly come to pass; and he sent and signified it by his angel unto his servant John.

Pageview Image Freiberg Hebrew Manuscript HS-314

חֲזוֹן יֵשׁוּעַ הַמָּשִׁיחַ אֲשֶׁר נָתַן לוֹ אֱלֹהִים כְּדֵי שֶׁיְּגַלֶּה לַעֲבָדָיו הַדְּבָרִים אֲשֶׁר צְרִיכִים שֶׁיַּעֲשׂוּ בִּזְמַן קָצוּר:

Hebrew Transcription

לוֹ	נָתַן	אֲשֶׁר	הַמָּשִׁיחַ	יֵשׁוּעַ	חֲזוֹן	Rev. 1:1
lo, " to him/it," (prep, 3ms)	natan "he/ it gave," (Pa'al/Qal, qatal, past 3ms)	asher, "which, that," (particle)	ha' maschiach, "the Messiah," (n ms)	Yeshua, (name)	chazon, "revelation, prophecy," (n ms constr)	Freiberg Manuscript HS-314

צְרִיכִים	אֲשֶׁר	הַדְּבָרִים	לַעֲבָדָיו	שֶׁיְּגַלֶּה	כְּדֵי	אֱלֹהִים
tzrichim, "necessary, required, must" (adj mp)	asher, " which, that,," (rel part)	ha' devarim, "the things," (n mp)	l' avadav, "to/ for/ his servants," (prep, n 3mp)	sh'y'galeh " who will reveal" (prep, v. Pi'el, yiqtol, fut, 3ms),	kedei, "in order to, to" (conj)	Elohim (name)

			קָצוּר	בִּזְמַן	שֶׁיַּעֲשׂוּ
			qatzor, "harvest," (n ms)	biz'man, "in/ with/ by (the) time of" (n ms constr)	sh' yei'asu, "that/ which/, be done," (prep, v. Nif'al, yiqtol, fut, 3mp)

Introduction

Miles R. Jones, PhD

"I am the Aleph and the Tav"

"I am the Alpha and the Omega" is what we read in English texts taken from the Greek. It seldom occurs to readers that many of the books in the New Testament were originally written in Hebrew - long before Greek-speaking believers became so numerous they dominated the Church. Therein lies the story of this book and what it reveals to us.

Revelation is called the ***Apocalypse*** in Greek, which comes from a long literary tradition in Hebrew. Numerous linguists who have analyzed the text - state unequivocally that the original text was Hebrew, the idioms are Hebrew, and the symbolism comes from the Hebrew Old Testament (***The Tanach***), as well as from other apocalyptic books in the Hebrew tradition. ***Revelation*** was originally written in Hebrew.

In both languages the two letters are the first and last of the alphabet, meaning - Yehovah is *"The First and the Last"* (Isaiah 41:4, 44:6, & 48:12). They also mean God is everything in between. The *Aleph Tav*, or *Alpha Omega*, are considered a title of the Almighty Himself. Here the parallels with Greek end. In Hebrew it also means that the alphabet itself is from Yehovah. Let that sink in.

There has only been one alphabet in human history. As different as they all look today - they all trace back to one single original alphabet that first appeared in the path of the Exodus at the time of the Exodus. Precursor inscriptions from Wadi al-Hol in Egypt, Luxor, Serabit alKhadim in the Sinai Peninsula, Mount Sinai in Midian in Arabia, and Joshua's Altar at Mount

7

Ebal in the Promised Land - all connect the dots of the Israelites' journey of the Exodus from Egypt to Israel. As a biblical archaeologist I have spent 20 years pursuing this evidence. The original alphabet of letters came from Mount Sinai.

That fascinating journey has led me step by step to the recovery of the lost manuscripts of the Hebrew *Brit Hadashah* - the New Testament. These manuscripts are not supposed to exist - but they do! The Benai Emunah Institute - which I direct - has tracked down, obtained, and authenticated some 48 Hebrew manuscripts of all or parts of the New Testament[2] - including six manuscripts of the book of *Revelation*.

The establishment of the Greco-Roman Church by Constantine in the fourth century has formed the battle lines between the Hebrew perspective and the Greek. The Greek Church and its descendants, including the Reformation churches, have all but obliterated the Hebrew perspective. Whatever the foundations of your faith - you deserve to know the original story. Any differences from the Greek have only served to strengthen my faith not weaken it.

One example serves to illustrate these differences. In Jeremiah 31:31 it speaks of a New Covenant relationship between Yehovah and His followers. Yeshua (Jesus) says in Matthew 26:28, "*This is my blood of the New Covenant which is poured out for many...*" That is from the Hebrew text. In the King James Version it says, "*This is my blood of the New Testament...*" That comes from the Greek text. In Hebrew, the books from Matthew to Revelation are called the *Brit Hadashah*, The New Covenant. In the Greek text from Matthew to Revelation, there is no New Covenant - it is called the New Testament. And so the Tanakh - the Old Covenant - becomes the Old Testament in Greek. Without understanding the covenant

---

[1] Evidence of the original alphabet is in *The Writing of God*.
[2] The tale of finding and authenticating *The Hebrew Gospels* is in the book *Sons of Zion vs Sons of Greece*.

relationship between Yehovah and His people, both in the Old and New Covenants, then Revelation is likely to forever be an undecipherable mystery to most.

There is a difference - a *covenant* **is a legally binding contract between God and His people - a** *testament* **is not.** The Greeks did not want to buy into the Torah with all of its strange laws and statutes. They considered it to be *"dead legalism!"* They wanted to create their own Greek doctrines, change the name of Yehovah to a Greek name (expressly forbidden in the Bible), change the name of His son to Greek; and, of course - have their own Scripture in Greek. **So, the Hebrew Covenant became a Greek Testament.** In modern times, many texts are going back to the original meaning - a good first step!

Hebrew Revelation 1:8 says, *"I am the Aleph and the Tav, the First and the Last, says Yehovah Elohim - Who is, Who was, and Who will be - the Almighty."* The Hebrew text uses the name of God, *Yehováh*, with the correct vowel pointing - as do so many Messianic texts.

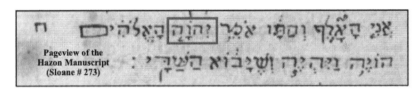

Pageview of the
Hazon Manuscript
(Sloane # 273)

This Preview Edition is different. It gives only the English translation of the twenty-two Hebrew chapters of the Book of Revelation. It is a compilation. From all the Hebrew texts of Revelation we have - we put together the first translation from the original Hebrew. Our team did magnificent work! The final decisions on what to include and how to phrase it are my responsibility. We will all stand before God for our deeds - any errors are mine alone to bear.

Our process has been to ascertain what the Spirit was telling us - through John. A lot of prayer went into this. Then we expressed it in the English language in the most clear and simple way possible without compromising the sense of the verse. We also stick as close as possible to the Hebrew wording.

Revelation 1:8

Hebrew Text Translation: **I am He *who is the First and the Last, the beginning and the end, says the Almighty,***

the One Who is, and Who was, and Who will be.

KJV: I am Alpha and Omega, the beginning and the ending, saith the Lord, which is, and which was, and which is to come, the Almighty.

Pageview Image Cambridge MS Oo.1.16.2

Pageview Image MS Gaster 1616

אמר	והסוף	תחילת	והאחרון	הראשון	הוא	אני
amar, "he/it said," (v. Pa'al/Qal, qatal, past, 3ms)	v' ha' sof, "and/ but/ so/ or the end," (n ms)	t'chilot, "beginning," (n ms)	v' ha' acharon, "and/ but/ so/ or (the) last", (n ms)	ha' rishon,"the first," (n ms)	hu, "he/ it," (3ms pron)	ani, "I," (1cs pron)

		ויהיה:	והוה	ההיה	אדיר	האדון
		v' yi'h'yeh, "and/ but/ so/ or he/it will be," (v. Pa'al/Qal, yiqtol, fut, 3ms)	v' hoveh, "and/ but/ so/ or who is," (ms)	ha' haya, "he/it was," (v. Pa'al/Qal, qatal, past, 3ms)	adir, "mighty, great, powerful," (adj ms)	ha' adon, "the LORD," (n ms)

Interlinear Chart

It has been the Benai Emunah Institute's mission to locate, obtain, authenticate, analyze, transcribe, translate and publish these Hebrew manuscripts of the *Brit Hadashah - The New Covenant*. By studying the differences between the Hebrew and the Greek we can identify the **markers of *The Hebrew Gospels*.** That means we try to find the historical origin of any change to the text in order to authenticate it. There are extensive examples and explanations of this process in my book *Sons of Zion vs Sons of Greece.*

The chart on the previous page represents our expanded formatting. The English translation of the Hebrew text is there along with the text of the King James Version (KJV) - always included for comparison. The KJV is the version coming from Greek. Then the Hebrew transcription of the letters and finally the Interlinear Chart so one can see the definition of each of the words. The archives of these Hebrew text translations will be open, for a subscription fee, to those who wish to dive deeper into the translation process. We will eventually have every one of the Hebrew *Brit Hadashah* manuscripts open to the public.

The symbolic and historical meaning of Revelation has been daunting to many readers. It is for that reason I believe many avoid the effort, deeming it so ambiguous as to be impossible to understand. There are, however, many things about the Book of Revelation that are perfectly clear, and often neglected. **It contains the only letters from Yeshua that we have - along with Yeshua's vision of the end times - a scenario of incredible importance and challenging symbolism!**

In the Cochin manuscripts of Revelation 1:8 (on a previous page), we see **the classic formulation of Yehovah's name which comes from the Hebrew verb "to be."**

יִהְיֶה	הֹוֶה	הָיָה	יְהֹוָה
Who will be	**Who is**	**Who was**	**Yehováh**

The name of Yehovah and His son Yeshua are both subjects of debate. This publication of the *Hebrew Book of Revelation* along with related research on the sacred Names should resolve that debate. Below are displayed the appearance of **the Sacred Name of Yehovah with correct vowel markings in ten manuscripts of <u>The Hebrew New Testament</u>!** It demonstrates the Messianic (Jewish-Christian) assemblies' desire to preserve and sanctify the true Name of Yehovah as directed by Yeshua in *The Hebrew Gospels* in John 17:6-26:

"I have manifested Your Name unto the men you have given me... I have declared unto them Your Name - and I will declare it!"

This was fulfillment of the prophecy in Psalms 22:22, **"I will declare Your Name to my brethren!"**

Thanks to Janice Baca for much of the research on the name of God.

Some Messianic scribes of *The Hebrew Gospels* continued to use substitute names for Yehovah as they had been instructed in their Hebrew yeshivas (schools). Having recovered four dozen manuscripts of all or part of *The Hebrew Gospels*, it is safe to say that many, if not most, **Messianic scribes courageously held to the Sacred Name *Yehováh* with the correct vowel pointing - despite it being banned by both the Judaic Church and the Greco-Roman Christian Church!** By now, thanks to the work of Nehemia Gordon in the Old Testament and my own research in the New Testament - there should be no more question. Unfortunately, ingrained views on this heated debate do not often go away with the mere discovery of evidence. It has become an article of faith to many. Sooner or later it will sort itself out. The evidence is definitive. Dr. Gordon has now discovered the Name of *Yehováh* with correct vowels in hundreds of manuscripts, thousands of times. I do not know of any instance of *Yahweh* with vowel pointing.

The debate also revolves around the correct given name of *Yeshua*, in Hebrew. Many scribes used the short (Aramaic) version *Yeshu*, while others attached the shortened root form of Yehovah's name *Yah*, or *Yahu*. This renders a variant name for Yeshua - *Yehoshua*. Some have even used the Grecian form of the name Yeshua with a final Greek /s/- *Yeshuas*. Here is the breakdown of their usage in Hebrew texts:

Freiburg 314, Neofiti 33, Augsburg, Yeates, Uppsala 31, Uppsala 32, Add.170, Shepreve 16.A.II, 2 Peter British Library, Vat Ebr 530, Udine Ebr 3,Marsaille MS 24-25	**Yeshua** used in 12 of 20 = **60%** manuscripts	יֵשׁוּעַ
Shem Tov Vat Ebr 101, Cambridge Oo.1.32, Guenzburg 363, Cambridge Oo.1.16.2, Matthew Russia Ms D101	**Yeshu** used in 5 of 20 mss =25%	יֵשׁוּ ישׁו
Sloane Hazon 273, Paris 131	**Yehoshua** used in 2 of 20 mss =10%	יְהוֹשֻׁעַ
HGC Vat Ebr 100	**Yeshuas** used in 1 of 20 mss = **5%**	ישׁואס

The text of *Hebrew Revelation* has some well-defined parameters in its symbolism. It begins with **seven letters** to the **seven Messianic congregations** in Asia Minor (now Turkey). Yeshua is the narrator of the divine vision given to his Apostle John. We first encounter Yeshua walking among **seven Menorahs**. Yeshua dictates the seven letters to **seven messengers (or angels)**. The vision opens with Yeshua breaking the **seven seals** of the book written by Yehovah himself. At the breaking of the last seal, there are **seven angels** who appear blowing **seven shofars**. At the last blowing of the seventh shofar, seven more angels appear with **seven bowls** (or vials) to be poured out on the earth to catastrophic effect, as well as **seven plagues**. At the end there is a **seven-day** marriage supper of the Lamb and his bride, the faithful remnant and those who have been martyred for his Covenant.

Usually missed in all this outpouring of symbolism are the **seven prophetic asides** - which are never explicitly mentioned in the text but do appear and they are critical. An aside is when one is telling a story and feels compelled to tell another story within the story, called an **aside**. The first of these asides comes in Rev. 7:1-17, the sealing of the 144,000 blessed ones. Another comes in between the opening of the sixth and seventh seals in Rev. 10:1-14. A great angel comes down from heaven with one foot on the land and one on the sea - and there are the **seven voices** of the **seven lightnings** - **seven thunders** - which John is forbidden to write down, leaving it an enduring mystery for us to decipher. The **seven prophetic asides** are key to following the   vision of *Revelation*. I will leave them for you to discover in the text.

The timing of the vision of *Revelation* is probably the chief hurdle to surmount in deciphering the symbolism of the text. There are three major approaches. They are the **Preterist, the Historical-Continuist, and the Futurist approaches.** Rev. 1:19 gives us a preview of this dilemma when Yeshua says to John, **"Write the things which you have seen, and the things**

which are, and the things which shall be hereafter." This is a perfect description of the historical-continuist approach. Some prophecy has already come to pass, some prophecy is happening now, and some prophecy is yet to come in the future.

The **Preterist** (Greek for *past*) approach is that of Eusebius - who rewrote the Bible - all prophecy has come to pass and "the end of prophecy" signals the return of the Messiah in his "conquering-king role." That is, of course, Emperor Constantine who ended the persecution of Gentile Christians and ruled over all the kingdoms of the earth.

Bishop Eusebius was the sycophant of Constantine who created for him a "divine right to rule" over all the earth justified from the Bible. There are few who accept Constantine as the return of the Messiah anymore, despite the fourth-century spin.

Nonetheless, it is quite clear the Apostles expected that the end times were upon them even in the first century. Yeshua's words seem to support that view. Indeed, their world did come crashing down with the destruction of the Temple in 79 AD and the destruction of Jerusalem in 125 AD. There had been a sporadic war of regular rebellions by the Jews against the Romans for a century and a half. Finally, the Romans razed Jerusalem and forbad their religion. The Romans salted the earth of Jerusalem so nothing would grow there. They crucified thousands at random until the rebellion stopped. All told the Romans killed a million and a half Israelites - about one third of Jews on the planet - the same proportion as were killed in the Holocaust. **It was certainly apocalyptic for all those of the first and second century!**

Many of us have been taught to be Futurists. It comes along with Replacement Theology. If you missed it in catechism - it means that all things promised to the chosen people, the Hebrews, now belong to the Gentile Church who have superseded the Judaic religion to become the new chosen people. There is plenty of differing opinions on Replacement Theology, also called Supersessionism. In this view, all the prophecy in *Revelation* is yet to come.

There is also the view that many of the things in Revelation are archetypal. For example, the seven churches are indicative of different situations, both bad and good, that happen within many churches. They are archetypes of wrong and right relation with Yehovah and Yeshua. There have certainly been these archetypes throughout history and along with them have come apocalypses aplenty over the centuries. The fall of empires have certainly been apocalyptic to those people living in those times. There has been no end of bloodshed. The world wars of the previous century were a killing ground of over a hundred million souls. Some would find it hard to imagine a catastrophe more grave than the toll of death and destruction worldwide in the past century. Unfortunately, now that we are equipped with nuclear weapons it is all too easy to imagine a worse outcome. Nonetheless, the weapons of Yehovah - earthquakes, hurricanes, plagues and famines can make our human weapons look like children's toys.

The revelations of this manuscript are enlightening, intriguing, and fascinating but they are also set in a context that is deeply grim for us to contemplate. Have we become so arrogant in our human pride that we think we can ignore Yehovah? Can we commit any iniquity on any scale no matter how horrific it is to God? It would seem that we believe we can. I have never seen the level of corruption and deceit and evil that I now see, not only in the country I live in, but in all the 'so-called' *civilized* nations of the world. I doubt that the reader of this book needs me to spell it out for them. Those of a spiritual nature can see what is happening. They are already asking themselves, "What is God trying to tell us?" "What does He want us to do?"

But many others do not see it, nor are they likely to be reading this book. "The natural man receives not the things of the Spirit of God - for they are foolishness unto him - neither can he know them, because they are spiritually discerned." (1 Cor. 2:14).

I leave you with many gems of the Spirit that have been uncovered in this text. Have you ever had a discussion of what happened to the lost Ark of the Covenant? I bet you have. The answer is in this book. Have you ever heard it discussed from the pulpit? I bet you haven't. The Greeks took the Covenant out of the Bible so they could write their own doctrines. In Revelation 11:19 in the Greek text it mentions the "ark of the testimony," which few recognize, so it goes in one ear and out the other. In the *Hebrew Book of Revelation* 11:19 says, **"The Temple of Yehovah was opened in heaven, and the <u>Ark of the tablets of the Covenant</u>* was revealed in His Temple - and coming *from it were thunder, lightning and great hailstones.*"**

In Rev. 15:5 the Ark of the Covenant is opened - and the seven plagues are released upon the earth! Has our ignorance, rebellion - or worse - rejection of the Almighty and his Law, opened a Pandora's box of woes and disasters upon our nations? God always warns us before bringing the hammer down. Maybe we should listen. **Is this the warning before the wrath of God comes upon us?**

I await the total eclipse of April 8th, 2024, the second eclipse to occur here within six months. I know this - I need to repent! We all need to repent for sliding into sin rather than following the eternal precepts of the Almighty.

Whether the axe is coming down right now or not - Repentance is our only hope - our path to Yehovah's salvation!

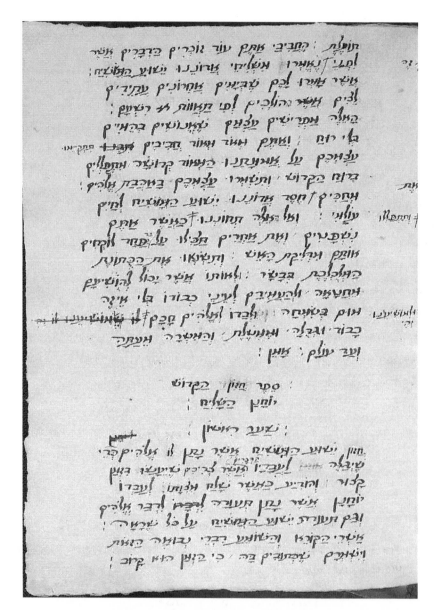

Chapter 1, Freiberg MS HS-314

Chapter 1

The Hebrew translation is given in **bold** - the King James Version
(KJV) is included for comparison.

1:1 The Revelation of Yeshua the Messiah, which Yehovah*
gave to him (John - Yohanan in Hebrew), to reveal to his
servants the things that they must do at the time of the
harvest.

> *Note: The abbreviation ה׳ (Ha-shem) is used in the Cambridge
> text as a substitute for the sacred name הוהי (Yehovah). The
> Gaster manuscript inserts םיהלא (Elohim) for הוהי (Yehovah).
> Yehovah, with the correct vowel pointing - is used in many,
> if not most, Messianic manuscripts. Therefore, the correct
> name of God, Yehovah, will be used whenever indicated in
> the Cambridge, or other manuscripts.

KJV: The Revelation of Jesus Christ which God gave unto him to
shew unto his servants which must shortly come to pass; and he sent
and signified *it* by his angel unto his servant John.

1:2 *Elohim* gave notice by his servant, John (Yochanan),
who delivered the Word of Yehovah, along with the
testimony of Yeshua the Messiah, about all that he saw.

KJV: Who bare record of the word of God, and of the testimony of
Jesus Christ, and of all things that he saw.

1:3 Blessed is the one who hears and proclaims the
words of this prophecy and keeps what is written in it -
for the time is near.

KJV: Blessed is he that readeth, and they that hear the words of this
prophecy, and keep those things which are written therein: for the time
is at hand.

19

Chapter 1, Cambridge Oo 1.16.2

1:4 I, John, who preceded the seven assemblies of Asia (Minor); grace and peace *to you*, from He - Who is, Who was, and Who will be - and from the seven spirits who stand before His throne.

KJV: John to the seven churches which are in Asia: Grace *be* unto you, and peace, from him which is, and which was, and which is to come; and from the seven spirits which are before his throne.

1:5 And from Yeshua the Messiah who is a faithful witness, the firstborn of the dead (saints), Head of kings of the earth - he who also loved us and washed us from our sins with his blood.

KJV: And from Jesus Christ, *who is* the faithful witness, *and* the first begotten of the dead, and the prince of the kings of the earth. Unto him that loved us, and washed us from our sins in his own blood.

1:6 *Yeshua* made us a kingdom* of priests unto Yehovah, his Father. To Him is the glory and dominion forever and for all time to come. Amen!

> *Note: This verse, along with Exodus 19:6 *"a kingdom of priests,"* and Revelation 12:10 *"Now... the kingdom of our God and the rule of His Messiah have come,"* make it clear that Yehovah is giving His authority to Yeshua not to human kings.

KJV: And hath made us kings and priests unto God and his Father; to him *be* glory and dominion for ever and ever. Amen.

1:7 Behold, *Yeshua* shall come in the cloud (with rejoicing). Every eye will see him. All who hurt him will mourn because of him. And so, all families of the earth *will* also. Amen!

> *Note: The word גָּנַ. *"rejoicing"* closely resembles the word וֹנַע *"cloud,"* however, it seems clear that the righteous will

הסודות

לעד : 22 וגם ארם תהיו רחמים : 23 אבל איזה מכם במעשים

טובים ותרחינו מן החשאים ; 24 אבל זה שיוכל לשמור אתכם בלי ס'

ספק ולעמוד אתכם לפני הארון בלי שום חטא : 25 לזה תהיה כבוד ית

ותפארת ומלכות מעולם ועד עולם אמן ;'

סוף מהאיגרת ששלה יודאס

אלה הסודות

נגלה על ידי יאהנניב

לעדת מילאנין

א פ

אלהמדסודות נתן אלהים לישו המשיח להראות לעבדיו מה

שיהיה בקרוב והוא שלח אותם על ידי מלאך שלו לעבדו יאהנניס:

2 העד לדיבור אלהים והעדות מישו המשיח ממה שראה : 3

קדוש הוא הקורא והשומעים זאת הנבואות ומקיימים מה שכתוב :

4 יאהנניס והשבעה זקנים באסיא חסד ישלוב יהיה עמכם מזה

שהיה והוה ויהיה, ומהשבעה רוחות שהמה מכסאו : 5 ומישו

המשיח העד הנאמן ויראשון שקם מרמתים ועיד ומצוה על הארץ ה'

האהברנו ורחיצרנו מעווינותינו עם דמו : 6 ועשה אותנו למלכים ול

ולכהנים לפני אליהם ואביו לו תהיה כבוד ותפארת מעולם ועד עולם

Chapter 1, Gaster 1616

rejoice upon the Messiah's return and the wicked, along with their 'kindred' spirits, will wail.

KJV: Behold, he cometh with clouds; and every eye shall see him, and they *also* which pierced him: and all kindreds of the earth shall wail because of him. Even so, Amen.

1:8 I am the Aleph and the Tav, the First and the Last, says Yehovah Elohim - Who is, Who was, and Who will be - the Almighty.*

> *Note: The Hebrew text clarifies we are speaking of Yehovah; whereas the KJV uses *"Lord"* (Jesus) *"which is to come"* rather than *"LORD (Yehovah, YHVH)"*. The *"Aleph Tav"* comes from the Hazon Ms., and *"Who is, Who was, Who will be"* comes from the Gaster manuscript.

KJV: I am Alpha and Omega, the beginning and the ending, saith the Lord, which is, and which was, and which is to come, the Almighty.

1:9 I am John - your brother - who shares in tribulation with you, and *who shares* in the kingdom, and who awaits upon Yeshua the Messiah. I was on the island, which is named Patmos, in the presence of the Word of Yehovah through the illumination of Yeshua.

KJV: I, John, who also am your brother, and companion in tribulation, and in the kingdom and patience of Jesus Christ, was in the isle that is called Patmos, for the word of God, and for the testimony of Jesus Christ.

1:10 Behold the Spirit soaked me at the beginning of the Sabbath*, and I heard a great voice** behind me like the voice of the trumpet.

> *Note: This was a correction in the margin, stating *"rotze leymor"* - 'as Scripture says' - "at the beginning of the Sabbath." The text said on *"yom shemesh"*, literally "the day of the sun".
>
> In the Greek it says *"on the Lord's Day"* (Sunday), which was

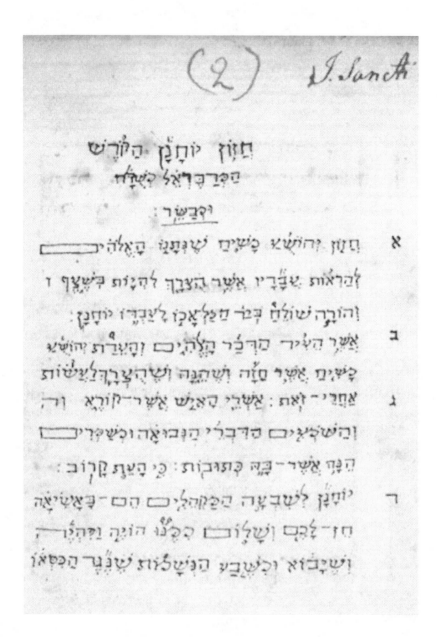

Chapter 1, Hazon-Sloane MS 273

added to validate Sunday worship - which was not instituted until centuries later. Clearly the scribe had a previous text of Hebrew Revelation different from the Greek.

**Note: This is a reference to the "*bat kol*" (the divine voice) which is a feminine noun - as is the Holy Spirit and the Shekinah - Glory of Yehovah's presence.

KJV: I was in the Spirit on the Lord's day, and heard behind me a great voice, as of a trumpet.

1:11 *The voice* **said to me; What you see, write in a book, and send it to the seven assemblies which are in Asia (Minor) - Ephesus, and Smyrna, and Pergamus and Thyatira and Sardis and Philadelphia and Laodicea!**

KJV: Saying, I am Alpha and Omega, the first and the last: and, What thou seest, write in a book, and send it unto the seven churches which are in Asia; unto Ephesus, and unto Smyrna, and unto Pergamos, and unto Thyatira, and unto Sardis, and unto Philadelphia, and unto Laodicea.

1:12 Behold, I turned to see the voice that was speaking with me, and from the moment I turned, behold I saw seven golden Menorahs.*

*Note: *"Menorah"* is mistranslated as *candlesticks* or *lampstands*, thus replacing, and erasing, the name **Menorah** in the Bible. The Menorah is a proper noun, the name of a specific icon created by Yehovah himself in Exodus 25:31-40. Changing a proper name into a common noun is a mistranslation.

KJV: And I turned to see the voice that spoke with me. And being turned, I saw seven golden candlesticks;

1:13 In the midst of the seven golden Menorahs, I saw someone like unto the Son of Adam (Man) who is dressed in a garment reaching down to his feet, girded about his chest with a golden sash.

KJV: And in the midst of the seven candlesticks *one* like unto the Son of man, clothed with a garment down to the foot, and girt about the paps with a golden girdle.

1:14 His head and his hair are white as wool, white like snow, and his eyes resemble a flame of fire.

KJV: His head and *his* hairs *were* white like wool, as white as snow; and his eyes *were* as a flame of fire;

1:15 His feet are like bronze from a fiery furnace, and his voice *is* like the sound of many waters.

KJV: And his feet like unto fine brass, as if they burned in a furnace; and his voice as the sound of many waters.

1:16   In his right hand *were* seven stars, and from his mouth went forth a two-edged sword,* and his face resembled the shining light of the sun in its strength.

> *Note: The *two-edged sword* is the Word of God, considered by some scholars to be both the old and the new covenants, two-edged, or as some have put it - the Torah and the Gospel. (Tom Bradford's Revelation series)

KJV: And he had in his right hand seven stars: and out of his mouth went a sharp two edged sword: and his countenance *was* as the sun shineth in his strength.

1:17 When I saw him, I fell at his feet as if dead. He laid his right hand upon me, saying, Do not fear, I am the First and the Last.*

> *Note*: "The First and the Last, the Beginning and the End"* are titles shared by Yehovah and Yeshua. See John 1:1, in the Hebrew, *"In the beginning was the Son, and the Son was with God and the Son was God"* so Yeshua indeed was - along with Yehovah - *"The First and the Last, the Beginning and the End."* See also Isaiah 41:4, 44:6, and 48:12.

KJV: And when I saw him, I fell at his feet as dead. And he laid his right hand upon me, saying unto me, Fear not; I am the First and the Last.

1:18 I am he who lives - but I was dead - and I was resurrected forever and ever. I have the keys of death and of Sheol.*

> *Note: Sheol means *underworld* in Hebrew, often translated into Greek as *Hades*, *Hell* in English.

KJV: I *am* he that liveth, and was dead; and, behold, I am alive for evermore, Amen; and have the keys of hell and of death.

1:19 In truth, write what you saw, and what is now, and what will be after this.*

> *Note: This is the classic description of the Historical-Continuist Theory of prophecy; some prophecy has already happened, some is happening now, and some is yet to be.

KJV: Write the things which thou hast seen, and the things which are, and the things which shall be hereafter;

1:20 *This is* the secret of the seven stars which you saw in my right hand, and the seven golden Menorahs. They are the seven messengers of *the* assemblies, and the seven Menorahs indicate the seven assemblies.

KJV: The mystery of the seven stars which thou sawest in my right hand, and the seven golden candlesticks. The seven stars are the angels of the seven churches: and the seven candlesticks which thou sawest are the seven churches.

Chapter 2

2:1 Write to the messenger of the assembly in Ephesus: Behold! He who holds the seven stars which are in his right hand - he who walks in the midst of the seven golden Menorahs - *it is* **he who says these things:**

KJV: Unto the angel of the church of Ephesus write; These things saith he that holdeth the seven stars in his right hand, who walketh in the midst of the seven golden candlesticks;

2:2 How *well* **I know your works and struggles, and your long suffering. I know that you do not tolerate evil people. You tested those that say they are apostles, but are not, and you found** *them* **liars!**

KJV: I know thy works, and thy labour, and thy patience, and how thou canst not bear them which are evil: and thou hast tried them which say they are apostles, and are not, and hast found them liars:

2:3 You sacrificed and suffered for the sake of my name (Yeshua) yet you did not fall from faith.

KJV: And hast borne, and hast patience, and for my name's sake hast laboured, and hast not fainted.

2:4 Nevertheless, in any case, I do have matters to bring against you because you have abandoned your first love (Torah).*

> *Note: Psalm 119:165 *"Great peace have they who love your Torah."* Psalm 119:97 *"O how I love your Torah!"* The commands to love the Torah are obscured by the fact the word *"Torah"* is removed from the Bible by translating it as *"law."*

1 John 3:4 *" Everyone who sins is violating Torah - indeed, sin is violation of Torah."* In the first century, some Messianic believers were falling away from Torah.

KJV: Nevertheless, I have somewhat against thee, because thou hast left thy first love.

2:5 Therefore, remember your *roots* from which you have grown away. Repent and return to your first works! If not, behold, I will come to you in haste, and I will remove your Menorah* from its place, if you will not repent.

> *Note: The Menorah and the tablets of stone bearing His Torah, both given at Mt. Sinai, are the *"tokens"* of Yehovah's authority (Exodus 3:12 & 25:31-40). So, Yeshua will remove their icon of authority to exist as an assembly of Yehovah, if they do not repent.

KJV: Remember therefore from whence thou art fallen, and repent, and do the first works; or else I will come unto thee quickly, and will remove thy candlestick out of his place, except thou repent.

2:6   But you still have this; that you hated the *pagan* works* of the Nicolaitans, which I also abhorred.

> *Note: The Nicolaitans were followers of Nicholas of Antioch, who came from paganism and, according to the early church fathers, included many pagan practices in his congregation. Verse 6 is entirely missing in the Cochin texts. It may be a later addition, because it is in the Hazon and Freiberg manuscripts.

KJV: But this thou hast, that thou hatest the deeds of the Nicolaitans, which I also hate.

2:7 Whoever has ears, let him hear what the Spirit says to the assemblies. Whoever overcomes - I will give to eat from the Tree of Life - which is in the Garden of Eden of my Elohim.*

*Note: This translation comes from the Gaster 1616 which says *"to eat"* from the Tree of Life.

KJV: He that hath an ear, let him hear what the Spirit saith unto the churches; To him that overcometh will I give to eat of the tree of life, which is in the midst of the paradise of God.

2:8 To the messenger of the assembly of Smyrna, write: Behold these words, says the First and the Last, who died and lives again.

KJV: And unto the angel of the church in Smyrna write; These things saith the first and the last, which was dead, and is alive;

2:9 *For* I, (Yeshua) I know your deeds and sorrows, and the blasphemy of those who say they are - *"people of Yehovah"* (Yehudim)* - Jews, but are not. They are the sons of Satan.*

*Note: The literal meaning of Yehudim is *'people of Yehovah,'* spelled *Judeans* in English. *Yahu* is one of the two short names for Yehovah, the other is *Yah*. Judea is the country named for Yehovah. Judeans are referred to as *'Jews.'* See Rev. 2:6 (on the Nicolaitans) and Romans 2:28-29 for further clarification.

KJV: I know thy works, and tribulation, and poverty, (but thou art rich) and I know the blasphemy of them which say they are Jews, and are not, but are the synagogue of Satan.

2:10 Do not fear them (sons of Satan). Behold! Satan will possess them in order to test you. The tribulation will last for ten days. *May you* be faithful until the day of your death, so that I may give to you the crown of life.

KJV: Fear none of those things which thou shalt suffer: behold, the devil shall cast some of you into prison, that ye may be tried; and ye shall have tribulation ten days: be thou faithful unto death, and I will give thee a crown of life.

2:11 Whoever has ears, let him hear what the Spirit says to the assemblies: Whoever overcomes will not find himself afflicted with the second death.*

> *Note: The second death is a spiritual death, being thrown into the lake of fire.

KJV: He that hath an ear, let him hear what the Spirit saith unto the churches; He that overcometh shall not be hurt of the second death.

2:12 Write to the messenger of the assembly of Pergamos, he who has the sharp two-edged sword in his hand says these things:

KJV: And to the angel of the church in Pergamos write; These things saith he which hath the sharp sword with two edges;

2:13 I know the place where you dwell. You dwell in the place *where* Satan is enthroned. Yet you still keep my name and you do not deny my faith. In *past* days, Antipas, my faithful witness, was killed near you, where Satan dwells.*

> *Note: The altar of the Temple at Pergamos was built in 184 BC by Eumenes II, of the Seleucid Greek dynasty. It was dedicated to Zeus and the pagan practices of the Greek gods of Olympia. During the persecution of Messianics, launched by Constantine in the fourth century AD and thereafter, many believers were executed (sacrificed) there at the altar of Satan. This altar and a reconstruction of the temple were in the Pergamon Museum in Berlin. Hitler used it as the model for his Nazi Nuremburg Palace. It was taken to the Soviet Union by Stalin after WWII where he proceeded to kill millions of his own citizens. I do not believe these most murderous events in human history were a coincidence.   Pergamon, which Revelation calls the throne, or altar, of Satan - was later returned to Berlin in 1958.

KJV: I know thy works, and where thou dwellest, *even* where Satan's seat *is*: and thou holdest fast my name, and hast not denied my faith, even in those days wherein Antipas *was* my faithful martyr, who was among you, where Satan dwelleth.

31

2:14 Still, I have matters to bring against you. There are those found among you who follow the teaching of Balaam*, who taught Balak to set a trap in the midst of the sons of Israel, to feast (revel) and commit whoredom.

> *Note: The entire story of Balaam is told in Numbers chapters 22, 23, 24, 25 & 31 as well as Rev 2:14. Also many had fallen away into the pagan practices of the Nicolaitans, see Rev. 2:6 & Rev. 2:15.

KJV: But I have a few things against thee, because thou hast there them that hold the doctrine of Balaam, who taught Balac to cast a stumbling block before the children of Israel, to eat things sacrificed unto idols, and to commit fornication.

2:15 Indeed, there are also found among you *those* who follow the teaching of the Nicolaitans.

KJV: So hast thou also them that hold the doctrine of the Nicolaitans, which thing I hate.

2:16 Therefore, repent, and if not, behold I will come in haste and I will fight with them (followers of Balaam & the Nicolaitans) with the sword of my mouth.*

> *Note: The two-edged sword coming from the mouth of Yeshua is the *"sword of the Spirit which is the Word of God."* Truth conquers.

KJV: Repent; or else I will come unto thee quickly, and will fight against them with the sword of my mouth.

2:17 Whoever has ears, hear what the Spirit says to the assemblies: Whoever overcomes - I will give *to him* the hidden manna - and I will give to him a <u>stone to build</u>* with my name written upon the stone - *a name* that no one knows - except *he* who accepts *it.*

> *Note: *"The name no one knows except he who accepts it"* -

may refer to the true name of Yehovah and His son Yeshua the Messiah. *"Knowing the name"* has a deep significance in Scripture. See Rev. 2:13, Exodus 33:12 & 33:17, and Acts 4:12. However, Yehovah has given new names to overcomers, Abram was changed to Abraham, Sarai to Sarah, Jacob to Israel. There is no white stone here - in this Hebrew text there is written testimony - the Name - hidden manna may be a reference to it.

KJV: He that hath an ear, let him hear what the Spirit saith unto the churches; To him that overcometh will I give to eat of the hidden manna, and will give him a white stone, and in the stone a new name written, which no man knoweth saving he that receiveth it.

2:18 And to the messenger of the assembly of Thyatira; write these words says the Son of Elohim - Who has eyes like a flame of fire, and feet resembling bronze burning in the furnace.

KJV: And unto the angel of the church in Thyatira write; These things saith the Son of God, who hath his eyes like unto a flame of fire, and his feet are like fine brass;

2:19 I know your works, and your faith and your love. Also, *I know* your intimacy (with God), and your service, and your latter works which are greater than the former.

KJV: I know your deeds, your love and faith, your service and perseverance, and that you are now doing more than you did at first.

2:20 Nonetheless, I have a few *things* against you, because you allow to remain *that* woman Jezebel. *She says she is a prophetess, but teaches falsely, misleading my servants to commit fornication, and eat of sacrifices to idols.**

> *Note: The many mystery cults of the first century would entice new followers by inviting them to a feast where animals were

sacrificed and dedicated to the pagan god(s) they followed. These feasts typically included drunkenness and fornication. That is why Scripture (Ex 34:15 & Acts 5:29) specifically forbids it.

KJV: Notwithstanding I have a few things against thee, because thou sufferest that woman Jezebel, which calleth herself a prophetess, to teach and to seduce my servants to commit fornication, and to eat things sacrificed unto idols.

2:21 I gave her (Jezebel) time to return in repentance, but she did not want to return from her fornication.

KJV: And I gave her space to repent of her fornication; and she repented not.

2:22 Behold, I banish her to a time of mourning, and those who commit fornication with her. They will be in great trouble if they do not repent regarding their deeds.

KJV: Behold, I will cast her into a bed, and them that commit adultery with her into great tribulation, except they repent of their deeds.

2:23 And her sons will die with death.¹ All the assemblies will know that I search hearts and minds.² I will give to each and every one of you according to *your* deeds.

> ¹Note: The repetition of *"die with death"* indicates emphasis in Hebrew.
> ²Note: The text means *"innermost parts,"* or more specifically the deepest emotions of the soul.

KJV: And I will kill her children with death; and all the churches shall know that I am he which searcheth the reins and hearts: and I will give unto every one of you according to your works.

2:24 I say to you, the others who *are* in Thyatira, who do not have the knowledge¹ (to interpret prophecy) -

and who do not know the depths of Satan - I will not send you another oracle.₂

> ₁Note: The Freiberg manuscript says *"teaching, knowledge or expertise,"* whereas other manuscripts say *"testimony, evidence, or proof."*
>
> ₂Note: The believers at Thyatira were led astray by the false oracle Jezebel because they did not have the knowledge to interpret and prove prophecy. Yeshua will not send another oracle since they have not the skill to prove prophecy true or not.

KJV: But unto you I say, and unto the rest in Thyatira, as many as have not this doctrine, and which have not known the depths of Satan, as they speak; I will put upon you none other burden.

2:25 But what you *have* now - hold on to - hold on until I come.

KJV: But that which ye have *already* hold fast till I come.

2:26 And to him (Yeshua)* who overcomes and stands fast until the end, I will give dominion over the nations.

> *Note: It is clear Yehovah has given dominion over the nations with an iron sceptre to Yeshua, not to men, see Revelation 19:11-16.

KJV: And he that overcometh, and keepeth my works unto the end, to him will I give power over the nations.

2:27 (Yeshua*)* will triumph *over* them (the nations) with a scepter of iron - *they will be* as earthen vessels* smashed like a battering-ram.

> Note: See Psalm 2:9: When an earthen vessel is not made correctly, the potter will shatter it. Daniel 2:44, *"And in the days of these kings shall the God of heaven set up a kingdom, which shall never be destroyed: and the kingdom shall not be left to other people, but **it shall break in pieces** and consume*

all these kingdoms, and it shall stand forever."

KJV: And he shall rule them with a rod of iron; as the vessels of a potter shall they be broken to shivers: even as I received of my Father.

2:28 As I received it from my Father* - "I will give to Him the morning star."

> *Note: These two final clauses of the chapter make sense together. When separated they make no sense at all. See Revelation 22:16 *"I am the root and the descendant of David, the bright morning star."* Yeshua is returning in homage to Yehovah what he has been given. All power and glory to God.

KJV: And I will give him the morning star.

2:29 Whoever has ears, hear what the Spirit says to the assemblies.

KJV: He that hath an ear, let him hear what the Spirit saith unto the churches.

Chapter 3

3:1 To the messenger of the church in Sardis write; These things, says he (Yeshua) who has the seven Spirits of (Yehovah), and the seven Stars; I know your works - because you have a name that you are alive - but behold *you* are dying.*

> Note: The church at Sardis has a name/reputation of walking in the Spirit, being *'alive'* in Yeshua, but now many are apparently slipping back into their secular ways and as a result becoming spiritually dead. See Psalm 91:14.

KJV: And unto the angel of the church in Sardis write; These things saith he that hath the seven Spirits of God, and the seven stars; I know thy works, that thou hast a name that thou livest, and art dead.

3:2 You must work diligently and stay strong about the *things within you* which are yet to die: For I have found that your mission before Yehovah is not yet finished.*

> Note: The Hebrew text is clear that it is not people dying here but the (things/issues) *sins* that have not yet been cleansed so these believers can complete their work.

KJV: Be watchful, and strong about the things which are ready to die: for I have not found thy works perfect before my God.

3:3 You yourself will remember when you took hold of the *Shema**, observed it, and made Teshuvah (repent and return to Yehovah): If you do not watch diligently, I (Yeshua) will come upon you like a thief (in the night), and you will not know the hour in which I will come.*

*Note: Yeshua declares the **Shema** in Matthew 22:37, *"Hear O Israel, Yehovah our Elohim - Yehovah is One. Blessed be your glorious kingdom, now and forevermore. You shall love Yehovah your Elohim with all your heart, all your soul, and all your might."* It is a command for believers to dedicate themselves completely to God and his Word. Yeshua commands Sardis to repent and return to Yehovah as they had in the beginning, because they have not finished their mission, and if they do not repent now, it may be too late for, they do not know when he will return. The Hebrew idiom *"like a thief in the night"* means *stealthily*.

KJV: "Remember therefore how thou hast received and heard, and hold fast, and repent. If therefore thou shalt not watch, I will come on thee as a thief, and thou shalt not know what hour I will come upon thee."

3:4 However, there are a few in Sardis who have not defiled their garments; and they shall walk with me (Yeshua) in white garments, because they are worthy.

KJV: Thou hast a few names even in Sardis which have not defiled their garments; and they shall walk with me in white: for they are worthy.

3:5 He who overcomes - he shall therefore be clothed in white raiment. Neither will I blot out his name from the book of life - instead - I (Yeshua) will praise his name before my Father, and before His angels.

KJV: He that overcometh, the same shall be clothed in white raiment; and I will not blot out his name out of the book of life, but I will confess his name before my Father, and before his angels.

3:6 He who has ears, *let him* hear what the Spirit will say unto the assemblies.

KJV: He that hath an ear, let him hear what the Spirit saith unto the churches.

3:7 To the messenger of the church of Philadelphia write, behold the things I say - who is holy and true - and has the key of David which opens what no one can shut thereafter, and closes what no one can open thereafter.*

*Note: See Isaiah 22:22 and Psalm 18.

KJV: And to the angel of the church in Philadelphia write; These things saith he that is holy, he that is true, he that hath the key of David, he that openeth, and no man shutteth; and shutteth, and no man openeth;

3:8 I know your works: Behold! I have set before you an open portal, which no one will be able to shut by any means. You have little strength, yet you have kept my Word, and you have not denied my name (Yeshua).

KJV: I know thy works: behold, I have set before thee an open door, and no man can shut it: for thou hast a little strength, and hast kept my word, and hast not denied my name.

3:9 I (Yeshua) will give notice *to* the assembly of Satan, *those* which say they are Yehudim (People of Yehovah)*, but are not, because they are liars! Behold I (Yeshua) will make them come in supplication - and they will bow at Your (Yehovah's) feet - and know that I (Yeshua) myself have loved You!

*Note: The word is *"Yehudim,"* which means *"Judeans"* but literally *"People of Yehovah,"* usually translated as *"Jews."* However, the word *"Jew"* was not recorded before AD 1000. See Revelation 2:9 in this text: *"I know... their slander, those who say they are 'People of Yehovah' (Yehudim) but they are not, because they are the sons of Satan!"* Some Messianics were bowing to the authority of the Rabbis' *"commandments of men"* rather than Yehovah. See Matthew 15:9 & 23:13.

KJV: Behold, I will make them of the synagogue of Satan, which say they are Jews, and are not, but do lie; behold, I will make them come and worship before thy feet, and to know that I have loved thee.

3:10 Since you have kept the gift of my word, *therefore*, I will keep you from the hour of temptation, which will come upon all the inhabitants *of* the land - to test all those who dwell in the earth.

KJV: Because thou hast kept the word of my patience, I also will keep thee from the hour of temptation, which shall come upon all the world, to try them that dwell upon the earth.

3:11 Behold, I (Yeshua) will come swiftly, *in* haste. Guard what you have (my Word) - *so* that no one will take your crown.

KJV: Behold, I come quickly: hold that fast which thou hast, that no man take thy crown.

3:12 He who overcomes, I will raise him up to stand in the temple of my God. He will go out no more. Also, I will write upon him the name of my Elohim and the name of the city of my Elohim - the New Jerusalem - which *is* descended from the heavens from my Elohim with my name.

KJV: Him that overcometh will I make a pillar in the temple of my God, and he shall go no more out: and I will write upon him the name of my God, and the name of the city of my God, *which is* new Jerusalem, which cometh down out of heaven from my God: and *I will write upon him* my new name.

3:13 Whoever has ears* (*to hear the truth*), let him hear what the Spirit will say to the assemblies.

> *Note: Analysis of the text makes it clear Yeshua is not talking about physical ears - but spiritual ears that are open to and seeking the truth. A closed mind/spirit will hear nothing it does not want to hear.

KJV: He that hath an ear, let him hear what the Spirit saith unto the churches.

3:14 And to the messenger of the assembly of Laodiceans, write these words said the Amen, the faithful and true witness, who is the first creation of Elohim.

KJV: And unto the angel of the church of the Laodiceans write; These things saith the Amen, the faithful and true witness, the beginning of the creation of God;

3:15 I know your deeds, that you are neither hot nor cold: O that you were either hot or, at least, cold!*

> *Note: Apparently, some believers were playing the political game trying to take both sides of every issue. God finds this abhorrent and dishonest, better to be wrong and honest, rather than lukewarm.

KJV: I know thy works, that thou art neither cold nor hot: I would thou wert cold or hot.

3:16 But since you are lukewarm, I will start to vomit you *out.*

KJV: So then because thou art lukewarm, and neither cold nor hot, I will spue thee out of my mouth.

3:17 Since you say "I am wealthy and made rich and do not need anything." Behold you do not know that you are poor and blind and naked!

KJV: Because thou sayest, I am rich, and increased with goods, and have need of nothing; and knowest not that thou art wretched, and miserable, and poor, and blind, and naked:

3:18 I counsel you to buy from me refined gold, so that you *too* will be refined, in order that you will be abundant, clothed in white clothing so that the nakedness of your stupidity will not be seen. And you will anoint your eyes so that you will see.

41

KJV: I counsel thee to buy of me gold tried in the fire, that thou mayest be rich; and white raiment, that thou mayest be clothed, and *that* the shame of thy nakedness do not appear; and anoint thine eyes with eye salve, that thou mayest see.

3:19 Since I, myself correct and chastise those that I love, in the same way be zealous and return in repentance *unto me* like this.

KJV: As many as I love, I rebuke and chasten: be zealous therefore, and repent.

3:20 Behold! I stand at the door knocking, and if he who will hear my voice, will open the door for me, I will come in unto him and eat the evening meal with him, and he with me.

KJV: Behold, I stand at the door, and knock: if any man hear my voice, and open the door, I will come in to him, and will sup with him, and he with me.

3:21 He who overcomes I will grant dominion to sit with me at my throne, even as I also overcame and sat with my Father at His throne.

KJV: To him that overcometh will I grant to sit with me in my throne, even as I also overcame, and am set down with my Father in his throne.

3:22 He who has ears (*to hear the truth*), let him hear what the Spirit will say unto the assemblies.

KJV: He that has an ear, let him hear what the Spirit said unto the churches.

Chapter 4

4:1 After these things, I looked, and behold there was a portal open in the heavens. The first voice I heard was as the sound of the shofar speaking with me, saying, "Come up, I implore you, and behold, I will show you what must happen soon."

KJV: After this I looked, and, behold, a door was opened in heaven: and the first voice which I heard was as it were of a trumpet talking with me; which said, Come up hither, and I will shew thee things which must be hereafter.

4:2   After these things I was in the Spirit, and behold, a throne was placed in the heavens, and the One who sits on the throne appeared.

KJV: And immediately I was in the spirit: and, behold, a throne was set in heaven, and *one* sat on the throne.

4:3 The one who sits on it (the throne), His face resembles a *precious* stone, *such as* jasper *or* ruby.   And a rainbow around the throne resembles an emerald.*

> *Note: See Exodus 24:10 referring to the appearance of Yehovah, *"there was under his feet as a paved work of a sapphire stone…"* Sapphires, and emeralds, come in a rainbow of different colors and shades.

KJV: And he that sat was to look upon like a jasper and a sardine stone: and *there was* a rainbow round about the throne, in sight like unto an emerald.

4:4 And around that throne were placed twenty-four

seats, and upon the seats sat twenty-four elders clothed in white raiment, and upon their heads, crowns of gold.

KJV: And round about the throne *were* four and twenty seats: and upon the seats I saw four and twenty elders sitting, clothed in white raiment; and they had on their heads crowns of gold.

4:5 And from the throne went forth lightning and thunder and flashes of fire. Seven burning lamps *were* before the throne, which are the seven Spirits of Elohim.

KJV: And out of the throne proceeded lightnings and thunderings and voices: and *there were* seven lamps of fire burning before the throne, which are the seven Spirits of God.

4:6 And before the throne, it was as a sea of glass, like unto crystal. In the midst of the throne, and around the throne, were four living creatures filled with eyes in front and back.*

> *Note: This is identical to the description of the appearance of Yehovah and His angels in Ezekiel chapter one. They are called *'chayaot'* in Ezekiel, *living ones*; translated as "*living creatures.*" Here, they are called "*bali chayim,*" *living lords*, meaning divinely created beings of authority - angels, perhaps - of Yehovah.

KJV: And before the throne *there was* a sea of glass like unto crystal; and in the midst of the throne and round about the throne, were four beasts full of eyes before and behind.

4:7 And the first living creature resembled a lion. And the second living creature resembled a young bullock. And the third living creature resembled the face of a man. And the fourth living creature resembled an eagle in flight.

KJV: And the first beast *was* like a lion, and the second beast like a calf, and the third beast had a face as a man, and the fourth beast *was* like a flying eagle.

4:8 Each and every one of the four living creatures has six wings roundabout, and are filled with eyes, and they will not rest day or night saying, "Holy! Holy! Holy! Elohim the Almighty who was, and is, and Who will be!"*

*Note: In the KJV & Freiberg it says *"was, and is, and is to come"* but in the Hebrew manuscripts - the Gaster and Cambridge it says *"Who was, Who is, and Who will be"* reflecting the fact that the name of Yehovah comes from the verb *"to be"* - so using *"to come"* is an aberration.

KJV: And the four beasts had each of them six wings about *him*; and *they were* full of eyes within: and they rest not day and night, saying, Holy, holy, holy, Lord God Almighty, which was, and is, and is to come.

4:9 These same living creatures gave honor and blessing to Him who sits on the throne, who lives forever and ever.

KJV: And when those beasts give glory and honour and thanks to him that sat on the throne, who liveth for ever and ever,

4:10 Behold, the twenty-four elders fell prostrate before the One who sits on the throne. They worshiped Him who lives forever and ever. They put the crowns from their heads before the throne, saying:

KJV: The four and twenty elders fall down before him that sat on the throne, and worship him that liveth for ever and ever, and cast their crowns before the throne, saying,

4:11 "I beseech You, Yehovah our Elohim*, You are worthy to bring the glory and the majesty and the might, as You have made all things, which by Your will they exist and were created."

*Note: In the text above the words "Adonai Elohim" Lord God were changed to *"Yehovah our Elohim."* It is clearly a

45

> Messianic belief to use the actual sacred name of Yehovah rather than substitute names.

KJV: Thou art worthy, O Lord, to receive glory and honour and power: for thou hast created all things, and by your desire they are and were created.

Chapter 5

5:1 I saw, in the right hand of the One (Yehovah) sitting upon the throne, a book written front and back, sealed with seven seals.*

> *Note: This description of *the "book"* mirrors Exodus 31:18, "two tablets… written with the finger of God," 32:15 "written on both sides, front and back," 32:16 *"the writing of God,"* Ex 32:32 *"your book (Yehovah) which you have written."* Exodus 40:3 describes the one-time ceremony of sealing those things going into the Ark - using the Menorah with its seven wax candles - presumably to make seven wax seals. Could this be the "book of the seven seals?"

KJV: "And I saw in the right hand of him that sat on the throne a book written within and on the backside, sealed with seven seals."

5:2 I saw a powerful angel calling out with a great voice, "Who, I pray you, is worthy to open the book and to break the seals?"

KJV: And I saw a strong angel proclaiming with a loud voice, Who is worthy to open the book, and to loose the seals thereof?

5:3 None was found that could open the book, detach its seals, and look at it - not in *the* heavens, nor on earth, nor under the earth.

KJV: And no man in heaven, nor in earth, neither under the earth, was able to open the book, neither to look thereon.

5:4 I wept bitterly because no one was found worthy to open the book and to look in it.

KJV: And I wept much, because no man was found worthy to open and to read the book, neither to look thereon.

5:5 One of the elders said to me, "Do not weep! Behold! The Lion of the tribe of Judah (*Yeshua*) - from the Root of David - overcame to open the book and to remove the seven seals.

KJV: And one of the elders saith unto me, Weep not: behold, the Lion of the tribe of Judah, the Root of David, hath prevailed to open the book, and to loose the seven seals thereof.

5:6 And behold, I saw - in the midst of the throne and the four living creatures, and in the midst of the twenty-four elders - a lamb standing, which had been slain* - who had seven horns and seven eyes that *are* the seven spirits of Elohim, which are sent over all the earth.

> Note: The wording from the Freiberg manuscript, גְרֶהֶן־וּלִיאָכ, *"as if it were slain,"* logically you cannot stand as if you were slain. The word וּלִיאָכ *keilu* also means *"in the role of."* The slain Lamb, (Yeshua appointed from the foundation of the world Rev. 13:8) is standing because he was resurrected.

KJV: And I beheld, and, lo, in the midst of the throne and of the four beasts, and in the midst of the elders, stood a Lamb as it had been slain, having seven horns and seven eyes, which are the seven Spirits of God sent forth into all the earth.

5:7 He came and he took the book from the right hand of the One sitting upon the throne.

KJV: And he came and took the book out of the right hand of him that sat upon the throne.

5:8 After that he (*Yeshua*) opened the book: Behold! The four divine living creatures* and the twenty-four elders prostrated themselves before the Lamb! In the

hand of each and every one are stringed instruments and bowls *made* of gold, full of sweet incense - which are the prayers of the holy ones.

> *Note: The Hebrew word used is יְלֵעַב םִייַח *baili chayim. Baili* means *'lord(s)'* as in husband, lord of the manor, or lord of a city/state, or a god. *Chayim* means *'living'*. In the context of Revelation these are clearly divine creatures, or beings, created by Yehovah to serve Him.

KJV: And when he had taken the book, the four beasts and four and twenty elders fell down before the Lamb, having every one of them harps, and golden vials full of odours, which are the prayers of saints.

5:9 They sang a new song, saying, "You, Adonai*, are worthy to take the book and to unlock the seals - because you were slain - our salvation, our deliverance is by your blood - for every tribe and tongue, for every people, and for every nation."

> *Note: *Adonai* refers to *"Lord"* (Yeshua), in this case, not *"LORD"* (Yehovah). *"LORD,"* in all capital letters is a translator's convention replacing the sacred name *Yehovah*.

KJV: And they sung a new song, saying, Thou art worthy to take the book, and to open the seals thereof: for thou wast slain, and hast redeemed us to God by thy blood out of every kindred, and tongue, and people, and nation.

5:10 You made us a kingdom of priests* for our Elohim, and we will reign over the earth.

> *Note: Exodus 19:5-6 says Yehovah will make his followers *"a kingdom of priests"*. This translation comes from the Paris Hebrew manuscript #131.

KJV: And hast made us unto our God kings and priests: and we shall reign on the earth.

5:11 I saw and I heard the sound of many angels around the throne and *divine* living creatures and elders, and their number was thousands of thousands.

KJV: And I beheld, and I heard the voice of many angels round about the throne and the beasts and the elders: and the number of them was ten thousand times ten thousand, and thousands of thousands;

5:12 They proclaimed with a loud voice to the lamb who was slain - you are worthy to receive power, divinity, strength, glory, and honor and blessing.

KJV: Saying with a loud voice, Worthy is the Lamb that was slain to receive power, and riches, and wisdom, and strength, and honour, and glory, and blessing.

5:13 From all creation which is in heaven and in earth, and under the earth, and who are in the sea, and in the midst of it - I heard all of them saying to Him Who sits on the throne and to the Lamb, "The blessing and glory and honor and dominion be forever and ever."

KJV: And every creature which is in heaven, and on the earth, and under the earth, and such as are in the sea, and all that are in them, heard I saying, Blessing, and honour, and glory, and power, be unto him that sitteth upon the throne, and unto the Lamb for ever and ever.

5:14 The four *divine* living creatures said, "Amen!" And the twenty-four elders fell upon their faces and worshiped the One Who lives forever and ever.

KJV: And the four beasts said, Amen. And the four and twenty elders fell down and worshiped him that liveth for ever and ever.

Chapter 6

6:1 When I saw that the Lamb *had* opened the first seal from the seven seals, I then heard one of the four *divine* living creatures, who said *in* a thunderous voice, "Come and see!"

KJV: And I saw when the Lamb opened one of the seals, and I heard, as it were the noise of thunder, one of the four beasts saying, Come and see.

6:2 I saw and beheld a white horse. He who sat upon it has a bow in his right hand. He was given a crown, and he went out so as to conquer, that he may overcome.

KJV: And I saw, and behold a white horse: and he that sat on him had a bow; and a crown was given unto him: and he went forth conquering, and to conquer.

6:3 After he opened the second seal, I heard the second *divine* living creature saying, "Come and see!"

KJV: And when he had opened the second seal, I heard the second beast say, Come and see.

6:4 Another horse went forth that was red. And he who sat upon it was given authority to take peace from the land, that a man would be able to put his neighbor to a violent death. A great sword was given to him.

KJV: And there went out another horse *that was* red: and *power* was given to him that sat thereon to take peace from the earth, and that they should kill one another: and there was given unto him a great sword.

6:5 When he (the Lamb - Yeshua) opened the third seal, I heard the third creature, who said, "Come and see!" And behold! - a black horse, and he who sat upon it had scales in his hand.

KJV: And when he had opened the third seal, I heard the third beast say, Come and see. And I beheld, and lo a black horse; and he that sat on him had a pair of balances in his hand.

6:6 And I heard a voice, in the midst of the four creatures, saying, "Behold! - two measures of wheat kernels in exchange for one small coin, and six measures of barley in exchange for one small coin. But do not *forget* to preserve the wine and the oil."

KJV: And I heard a voice in the midst of the four beasts say, A measure of wheat for a penny, and three measures of barley for a penny; and *see* thou hurt not the oil and the wine.

6:7 When he (Yeshua) opened the fourth seal, I heard the voice of the fourth creature, saying, "Come and see!"

KJV: And when he had opened the fourth seal, I heard the voice of the fourth beast say, Come and see.

6:8 Behold! - a dappled horse, and he who sat upon it was named Death, and She'ol (Hell) followed after him. He was given power over the four corners of the earth - to cause death with the sword, with famine and with pestilence against the living creatures on the earth.

KJV: And I looked, and behold a pale horse: and his name that sat on him was Death, and Hell followed with him. And power was given unto them over the fourth part of the earth, to kill with sword, and with hunger, and with death, and with the beasts of the earth.

6:9 When he had opened the fifth seal, I saw under the altar the souls of those slain because of the word of

Yehovah - and because of their testimony.

KJV: "And when he had opened the fifth seal, I saw under the altar the souls of them that were slain for the word of God, and for the testimony which they held:"

6:10   They cried out in a great voice saying, "How long, blessed Lord, until you judge and take vengeance for our blood, *shed* by the hand of those who dwell upon the earth?"

KJV: And they cried with a loud voice, saying, How long, O Lord, holy and true, dost thou not judge and avenge our blood on them that dwell on the earth?

6:11   They will all be given - each and every one - white garments.   It was said to them that they may rest until the time of the harvest, until the number of their friends and brothers that will be martyred shall be fulfilled.

KJV: And white robes were given unto every one of them; and it was said unto them, that they should rest yet for a little season, until their fellow servants also and their brethren, that should be killed as they *were*, should be fulfilled.

6:12 When he opened the sixth seal, I saw a great deafening earthquake. The sun became black like sackcloth made from goats' hair. The whiteness of the moon became as blood!

KJV: And I beheld when he had opened the sixth seal, and, lo, there was a great earthquake; and the sun became black as sackcloth of hair, and the moon became as blood;.

6:13 The stars fell from the heavens to the earth, like a fig tree casting off its figs when shaken by a great wind.

KJV: And the stars of heaven fell unto the earth, even as a fig tree casteth her untimely figs, when she is shaken of a mighty wind.

6:14 The heavens were pushed away from their places, like a scroll when rolled up. Every mountain and every island was shaken.

KJV: And the heaven departed as a scroll when it is rolled together; and every mountain and island were moved out of their places.

6:15 The kings of the earth, the officers, the tribes, the rich, the powerful, and every servant and freeman hid themselves in caves, and commanded the mountains:

KJV: And the kings of the earth, and the great men, and the rich men, and the chief captains, and the mighty men, and every bondman, and every free man, hid themselves in the dens and in the rocks of the mountains;

6:16 Saying to the mountains and the cliffs, "Cause yourselves to fall on us and hide us from the eyes of Him who is dwelling upon the throne, and from the anger of the Lamb,

KJV: And said to the mountains and rocks, Fall on us, and hide us from the face of him that sitteth on the throne, and from the wrath of the Lamb:

6:17 because the great day of His wrath has come!" But who is able to stand?

KJV: For the great day of his wrath is come; and who shall be able to stand?

Chapter 7

7:1 After this I saw four angels standing upon *the* four corners of the earth, restraining in their hands the four winds of the earth, that they should not blow upon the land or upon the sea or upon any tree.

KJV: And after these things I saw four angels standing on the four corners of the earth, holding the four winds of the earth, that the wind should not blow on the earth, nor on the sea, nor on any tree.

7:2 Afterward I saw a messenger from the angels ascending from the east of the sun - who had the seal of the living El (Elohim). He called out with a great voice to the four angels, which were given authority to destroy the land and the sea.

KJV: And I saw another angel ascending from the east, having the seal of the living God: and he cried with a loud voice to the four angels, to whom it was given to hurt the earth and the sea,

7:3 The (Voice) said, "Do not damage the land nor the sea, nor even a tree, until we have marked a *Tav** (sign) on the foreheads of the servants of Yehovah."

> *Note: For thousands of years, the letter Tav from the paleo-Hebrew alphabet was a cross, see Ez 9:4-6.

KJV: saying, Hurt not the earth, neither the sea, nor the trees, till we have sealed the servants of our God in their foreheads.

7:4   I heard the number of them who had been marked by Him, and they will be 144,000 from all the tribes of the sons of Israel.

KJV: And I heard the number of them which were sealed: *and there were* sealed an hundred *and* forty *and* four thousand of all the tribes of the children of Israel.

7:5 From the tribe of Yehudah (Judah) 12,000 were marked. Of the tribe of Rueben 12,000 were marked. Of the tribe of Gad 12,000 were marked.

KJV: Of the tribe of Judah *were* sealed twelve thousand. Of the tribe of Reuben *were* sealed twelve thousand. Of the tribe of Gad *were* sealed twelve thousand.

7:6 From the tribe of Asher 12,000 were marked. Of the tribe of Naphtali 12,000 were marked. From the tribe of Menasheh 12,000 were marked.

KJV: Of the tribe of Aser *were* sealed twelve thousand. Of the tribe of Nepthalim *were* sealed twelve thousand. Of the tribe of Manasses *were* sealed twelve thousand.

7:7 From the tribe of Shimon 12,000 were marked. Of the tribe of Levi 12,000 were marked. From the tribe of Yissaschar 12,000 were marked.

KJV: Of the tribe of Simeon *were* sealed twelve thousand. Of the tribe of Levi *were* sealed twelve thousand. Of the tribe of Issachar *were* sealed twelve thousand.

7:8 From the tribe of Zevulun 12,000 were marked. Of the tribe of Yosef 12,000 were marked. Of the tribe of Bin'yamin 12,000 were marked.

KJV: Of the tribe of Zabulon *were* sealed twelve thousand. Of the tribe of Joseph *were* sealed twelve thousand. Of the tribe of Benjamin *were* sealed twelve thousand.

7:9 After that I saw a great multitude that could not be numbered from all nations, and families, and people,

and tongues standing before the throne - in front of the eyes of the Lamb - clothed in white robes with palm branches in their hands.

KJV: After this I beheld, and, lo, a great multitude, which no man could number, of all nations, and kindreds, and people, and tongues, stood before the throne, and before the Lamb, clothed with white robes, and palms in their hands;

7:10 They cried out with a great voice, "Salvation to those belonging to Yehovah - who sits upon the throne - and unto the Lamb!"

KJV: And cried with a loud voice, saying, Salvation to our God which sitteth upon the throne, and unto the Lamb.

7:11 The angels standing around the throne, also the elders, and the four *divine* living creatures - fell upon their faces, worshiping before the throne of Yehovah.

KJV: And all the angels stood round about the throne, and *about* the elders and the four beasts, and fell before the throne on their faces, and worshipped God,

7:12 They said, "So may it be! The blessing, and might, and strength, be unto our Elohim for ever and ever! Amen!

KJV: Saying, Amen: Blessing, and glory, and wisdom, and thanksgiving, and honour, and power, and might, *be* unto our God for ever and ever. Amen.

7:13 One of the elders answered and said to me, "Behold, those dressed in white robes - who are these, or rather, where are they from?"

KJV: And one of the elders answered, saying unto me, What are these which are arrayed in white robes? and whence came they?

7:14 I (John) said unto him, "My lord, excuse me - *but* you know!" And he said to me, "Behold! These are the ones who came out of great tribulation and have washed and purified their robes - and made them white by the blood of the Lamb."

KJV: And I said unto him, Sir, thou knowest. And he said to me, These are they which came out of great tribulation, and have washed their robes, and made them white in the blood of the Lamb.

7:15 "For this reason they are before the throne of Yehovah - having been consecrated in His Temple, they are serving Him day and night. He who sits upon the throne will dwell among them."

KJV: Therefore are they before the throne of God, and serve him day and night in his temple: and he that sitteth on the throne shall dwell among them.

7:16 "They will not hunger nor thirst, nor be afflicted by the scorching heat of the sun."

KJV: They shall hunger no more, neither thirst any more; neither shall the sun light on them, nor any heat.

7:17 "For the Lamb will lead them, *saying*, 'Come to the Water of Life!' Yehovah Elohim will wipe all tears from their eyes."

KJV: For the Lamb which is in the midst of the throne shall feed them, and shall lead them unto living fountains of waters: and God shall wipe away all tears from their eyes.

Chapter 8

8:1 When he opened the seventh seal: behold, all became silent in heaven for an hour.

KJV: And when he had opened the seventh seal, there was silence in heaven about the space of half an hour.

8:2 Then I saw seven angels standing before Yehovah, and they were given seven shofars.

KJV: And I saw the seven angels which stood before God, and to them were given seven trumpets.

8:3 Another angel came and he stood before the altar, having a censer of gold; and they gave him much incense to deliver prayers of all the holy ones upon the altar of gold, which is before the throne.

KJV: And another angel came and stood at the altar, having a golden censer; and there was given unto him much incense, that he should offer it with the prayers of all saints upon the golden altar which was before the throne.

8:4 And the smoke from the incense rose up with the prayers of the holy ones, from the hand of the angel who was before Yehovah.

KJV: And the smoke of the incense, which came with the prayers of the saints, ascended up before God out of the angel›s hand.

8:5 And the angel took the golden censer, and he filled it with the altar's fire, and he threw it to the earth. Then the

sounds became a deafening thunder, and lightning, and an earthquake.

KJV: And the angel took the censer, and filled it with fire of the altar, and cast *it* into the earth: and there were voices, and thunderings, and lightnings, and an earthquake.

8:6 The seven angels with the seven shofars were prepared to sound their shofars.

KJV: And the seven angels which had the seven trumpets prepared themselves to sound.

8:7 And the first angel sounded the shofar and there was hail, and fire mixed with blood, and it fell upon the earth. A third of the trees burned, and all the greenery burned.

KJV: The first angel sounded, and there followed hail and fire mingled with blood, and they were cast upon the earth: and the third part of trees was burnt up, and all green grass was burnt up

8:8   Then the second angel sounded the shofar, and the great mountain burning with fire fell into the sea, and a third of the sea became as blood.

KJV: And the second angel sounded, and as it were a great mountain burning with fire was cast into the sea: and the third part of the sea became blood;

8:9 A third of the creatures which were alive in the sea - died - and a third of the ships were lost.

KJV: And the third part of the creatures which were in the sea, and had life, died; and the third part of the ships were destroyed.

8:10   The third angel sounded the shofar, and there fell from heaven a great star, burning like a torch, and it fell into a third of the rivers and wells of water.

KJV: And the third angel sounded, and there fell a great star from heaven, burning as it were a lamp, and it fell upon the third part of the rivers, and upon the fountains of waters;

8:11 The name of the star was Wormwood*, and a third of the water turned scarlet, and many people died from the water because it turned bitter.

*Note: Two different words are used in the Hebrew texts, *"tola'at"* which refers to the Scarlet Worm which lays eggs in the bark of trees producing a scarlet dye staining the wood, thus the translation *'wormwood.'* The Scarlet Worm dye is bitter which leads to the second word usage *"la'anah"* meaning bitter. So, the water turned scarlet and bitter from the wormwood.

KJV: And the name of the star is called Wormwood: and the third part of the waters became wormwood; and many men died of the waters, because they were made bitter.

8:12 Then the fourth angel sounded the shofar - and a third of the sun, the moon, and the stars became eclipsed, that third would not shine, neither by night nor by day.

KJV: And the fourth angel sounded, and the third part of the sun was smitten, and the third part of the moon, and the third part of the stars; so as the third part of them was darkened, and the day shone not for a third part of it, and the night likewise.

8:13 And I saw and heard the sound of an angel who hovered in the heavens saying, "Oi, Oi, Oi, to those dwelling upon the earth - because of the clarion calls of the last three angels who have yet to sound their shofars."

KJV: And I beheld, and heard an angel flying through the midst of heaven, saying with a loud voice, Woe, woe, woe, to the inhabiters of the earth by reason of the other voices of the trumpet of the three angels, which are yet to sound!

Chapter 9

9:1 And the fifth angel sounded the shofar, and I saw a star from heaven fall upon the earth. The key to the deep was given to him (the fifth angel).

KJV: And the fifth angel sounded, and I saw a star fall from heaven unto the earth: and to him was given the key of the bottomless pit.

9:2 He opened the pit of the deep, and smoke from the pit rose like smoke from a great furnace, the sun and the air were darkened by the smoke of the pit.

KJV: And he opened the bottomless pit; and there arose a smoke out of the pit, as the smoke of a great furnace; and the sun and the air were darkened by reason of the smoke of the pit.

9:3 Out of the smoke of the pit - locusts came out upon *the* earth and they were given dominion, as the scorpions were given dominion on earth.

KJV: And there came out of the smoke locusts upon the earth: and unto them was given power, as the scorpions of the earth have power.

9:4 They were commanded not to destroy the grass of the earth, nor any green plant, nor any tree, but only (to attack) the people who do not have the seal of Yehovah on their foreheads.

KJV: And it was commanded them that they should not hurt the grass of the earth, neither any green thing, neither any tree; but only those men which have not the seal of God in their foreheads.

9:5 No authority was given to them to kill people, but only to grieve them for five months - with the sting of scorpions they would torment mankind.

KJV: And to them it was given that they should not kill them, but that they should be tormented five months: and their torment was as the torment of a scorpion, when he striketh a man.

9:6 In those days, men will seek death, but will not find it. They will greatly yearn to die, but death will flee from them.

KJV: And in those days shall men seek death, and shall not find it; and shall desire to die, and death shall flee from them.

9:7 The locusts resembled warhorses prepared for battle. Upon their heads were a likeness crowned with gold* - and their faces were like the faces of men.

> *Note: There are locusts that have a golden head, which resemble golden crowns. They had the tails of scorpions and with their long legs were like unto warhorses going into battle.

KJV: And the shapes of the locusts were like unto horses prepared unto battle; and on their heads were as it were crowns like gold, and their faces were as the faces of men.

9:8 Their hair was *fine* like the hair of women. Their teeth were like the teeth of lions.

KJV: And they had hair as the hair of women, and their teeth were as the teeth of lions.

9:9 They had body armor, resembling iron breastplates, and the sound of their wings was like *the* sound of chariot horses charging into battle.

KJV: And they had breastplates, as it were breastplates of iron; and the sound of their wings was as the sound of chariots of many horses running to battle.

9:10 They had tails like scorpions. They stung with their tails those under their power - to torment people for a duration of five months.

KJV: And they had tails like unto scorpions, and there were stings in their tails: and their power was to hurt men five months.

9:11 They had their king, the angel of the abyss, whose name in Hebrew is Abaddon, and in the Greek tongue, Apollyon, and in the Roman tongue, Terminus.

KJV: And they had a king over them, which is the angel of the bottomless pit, whose name in the Hebrew tongue is Abaddon, but in the Greek tongue hath his name Apollyon.

9:12 One woe has passed. Behold! Two more woes are coming!

KJV: One woe is past; and, behold, there come two woes more hereafter.

9:13 The sixth angel sounded the shofar, and I heard a voice coming from the light* of the golden altar, which is before Yehovah.

> *Note: This word *"qeren"* in Hebrew means *light* or *horn*, as a result it is often mistranslated. See 1st Kings 1:50-51 and 1st Kings 2:28. As far as the heavenly altar - there may well have been both - golden horns on the four corners and a heavenly light coming from the altar.

KJV: And the sixth angel sounded, and I heard a voice from the four horns of the golden altar which is before God,

9:14 (The Voice) said to the sixth angel with the shofar, "Loose the four (fallen) angels which are bound under the great river Euphrates."

KJV: Saying to the sixth angel which had the trumpet, Loose the four angels which are bound in the great river Euphrates.

9:15 The four (fallen) angels were let loose - who had been prepared for the hour, for the day, for the month, and for the year - to kill a third of mankind.

> *Note: It is presumed these are the fallen angels of Satan - Yehovah uses them to achieve his ends.

KJV: And the four angels were loosed, which were prepared for an hour, and a day, and a month, and a year, for to slay the third part of men.

9:16 And the number of *their* army of horsemen was twenty times ten thousand, and I heard their number, 200,000.*

> *Note: The numbers differ in other verses, so we can only be certain that there was a huge number.

KJV: And the number of the army of the horsemen were two hundred thousand thousand: and I heard the number of them.

9:17 And so I saw the vision of the horses, and those who sat on them had body armor of fire, brimstone, and sulfur. The heads of the horses were like the heads of lions. Out of their mouths came fire, smoke, and brimstone.

KJV: And thus I saw the horses in the vision, and them that sat on them, having breastplates of fire, and of jacinth, and brimstone: and the heads of the horses were as the heads of lions; and out of their mouths issued fire and smoke and brimstone.

9:18 And by these three plagues, (*fire, smoke, brimstone*) a third of the sons of mankind were killed.

KJV: By these three was the third part of men killed, by the fire, and by the smoke, and by the brimstone, which issued out of their mouths.

9:19 The power of the horses is in their mouths and in their tails. Their tails are like serpents, with which they kill!

KJV: For their power is in their mouth, and in their tails: for their tails were like unto serpents, and had heads, and with them they do hurt.

9:20 Nonetheless, there were many children of mankind who cannot be put to death by these strikes - because they repented of their evil deeds. They do not pray to Satan nor to idols of clay, stone, wood, silver, or gold - which are not able to walk or speak or hear.

> *Note: The word repentance comes from the noun "teshuvah" which means to repent and return to Yehovah. This translation differs greatly from the Greek as shown in the KJV!

KJV: And the rest of the men which were not killed by these plagues yet repented not of the works of their hands, that they should not worship devils, and idols of gold, and silver, and brass, and stone, and of wood: which neither can see, nor hear, nor walk:

9:21 There are *still* those who did not repent of their murders, nor of their sorceries, nor of their fornications, *nor* of their thefts. They shall not die a natural death!

KJV: Neither repented they of their murders, nor of their sorceries, nor of their fornication, nor of their thefts.

Chapter 10

10:1 I saw another mighty angel who came down from the heavens, clothed in a cloud, and there was a rainbow upon his head. His face was like the sun, and his feet were like pillars of fire.

KJV: And I saw another mighty angel come down from heaven, clothed with a cloud: and a rainbow was upon his head, and his face was as it were the sun, and his feet *were* as pillars of fire:

10:2 He had an open book in his hand, and put his right foot on the sea, and his left foot on the earth.

KJV: And he had in his hand a little book open: and he set his right foot upon the sea, and his left foot on the earth,

10:3 He called out with a great voice like unto the lion roaring, and as he called out, the seven voices of the lightnings thundered their words.*

> **Note: In Revelation 10:5 the angel raises his hands to the heavens, the angel is calling down the lightning and thunder, the voice of the heavens.*

KJV: And cried with a loud voice, as when a lion roareth: and when he had cried, seven thunders uttered their voices.

10:4 After the voices of the seven lightnings spoke their words - I wanted to write - but lo! I heard a divine voice from the heavens say to me, "Seal that which the voices of the seven lightnings spoke, and do not write their words!"

Note: The *"bat kol" divine voice* comes from the Cochin manuscripts.

KJV: And when the seven thunders had uttered their voices, I was about to write: and I heard a voice from heaven saying unto me, Seal up those things which the seven thunders uttered, and write them not.

10:5 The angel - which I saw standing on the sea and on the earth - he lifted his hands to the heavens.

KJV: And the angel which I saw stand upon the sea and upon the earth lifted up his hand to heaven,

10:6 He swore by the Eternal Living One, who created the heavens and all that exists - the earth, the sea, and all that is in them - "There is no more time!"

KJV: And sware by him that liveth for ever and ever, who created heaven, and the things that therein are, and the earth, and the things that therein are, and the sea, and the things which are therein, that there should be time no longer:

10:7 Once the seventh angel blows his shofar - all the secrets of Yehovah will be accomplished - just as He revealed by the hand of the prophets, His servants!

Note: In Revelation there are seven Menorahs, seven letters to the seven churches, seven seals, seven shofars, seven bowls (or vials) - but amongst all this **there are also seven prophetic pauses or asides** - the pause in this narrative reveals the voices of seven lightnings, in-between the sounding of the sixth shofar and the seventh shofar which is yet to come in Revelation 11:15, twenty-five verses later.

KJV: But in the days of the voice of the seventh angel, when he shall begin to sound, the mystery of God should be finished, as he hath declared to his servants the prophets.

10:8 I heard again the divine voice saying to me, "Go

and take the open book from the hand of the angel who stands on the sea and the earth."

KJV: And the voice which I heard from heaven spake unto me again, and said, Go and take the little book which is open in the hand of the angel which standeth upon the sea and upon the earth.

10:9 So I went to the angel and said to him, "Please give me the book!" And he said to me, "Take the book and swallow it, for it will be like honey in your mouth - but bitter in your bowels."

KJV: And I went unto the angel, and said unto him, Give me the little book. And he said unto me, Take it, and eat it up; and it shall make thy belly bitter, but it shall be in thy mouth sweet as honey.

10:10 I took the book from the angel's hand, and I swallowed it, and it was sweet like honey in my mouth - but when I swallowed it, behold, it became bitter in my stomach.

KJV: And I took the little book out of the angel's hand, and ate it up; and it was in my mouth sweet as honey: and as soon as I had eaten it, my belly was bitter.

10:11 Then he said to me, "Behold, You must prophesy again to nations, peoples and to sovereigns."

KJV: And he said unto me, Thou must prophesy again before many peoples, and nations, and tongues, and kings.

Chapter 11

11:1 There was given me a reed like unto a rod*, and it was said to me - Arise and measure the temple of Yehovah and the altar, and those who pray therein.

> *Note: The 'reed' was a measuring rod - probably a "cubit" - typically the length of the forearm.

KJV: And there was given me a reed like unto a rod: and the angel stood, saying, Rise, and measure the temple of God, and the altar, and them that worship therein.

11:2 The courtyard which is outside the temple - do not measure it! For forty-two months (lunar cycles) it has been given to the nations to trample the Holy City.

KJV: But the court which is without the temple leave out, and measure it not; for it is given unto the Gentiles: and the holy city shall they tread under foot forty and two months.

11:3 And I will give my two witnesses to prophesy 1,260 days, wearing sackcloth.

KJV: And I will give *power* unto my two witnesses, and they shall prophesy a thousand two hundred *and* threescore days, clothed in sackcloth.

11:4 These are the two olive trees, and the two Menorahs, standing before the Elohim of the earth.

> Note: This is a reference to Zachariah 4:14, "These are the two anointed ones (Messiahs), that stand before the God of all the earth." Often cited as the two witnesses in Rev. 11:3-12, Moses & Elijah.

KJV: These are the two olive trees, and the two candlesticks standing before the God of the earth.

11:5 If anyone wants to harm these two, behold, fire will come out from their mouths and will devour their enemies - and they will be slain.

KJV: And if any man will hurt them, fire proceedeth out of their mouth, and devoureth their enemies: and if any man will hurt them, he must in this manner be killed.

11:6 They have the power to shut the heavens so that there will be no rain during the days of their prophecy. They also have the power over the waters to turn them into blood, and to smite the earth with all *sorts of* plagues as they will.

KJV: These have power to shut heaven, that it rain not in the days of their prophecy: and have power over waters to turn them to blood, and to smite the earth with all plagues, as often as they will.

11:7 When they have finished their prophecy, behold, the beast will come up from the abyss and make war against them. He will defeat them and kill them.

KJV: And when they shall have finished their testimony, the beast that ascendeth out of the bottomless pit shall make war against them, and shall overcome them, and kill them.

11:8 Their corpses will be thrown into the streets of the Holy City - which is called the spirit of Sodom and Egypt - because there our Lord was crucified.

KJV: And their dead bodies *shall lie* in the street of the great city, which spiritually is called Sodom and Egypt, where also our Lord was crucified.

11:9 And the nations will see their corpses for a duration

of three and a half days - and they shall not be buried.

KJV: And they of the people and kindreds and tongues and nations shall see their dead bodies three days and an half, and shall not suffer their dead bodies to be put in graves.

11:10 Some on the earth will rejoice over them (& their death). They will send gifts one to another because these two prophets brought grief to *many** residing upon the earth.

> *Note: The evil and unrepentant have been persecuted, they are delighted in the death of God's prophets.

KJV: And they that dwell upon the earth shall rejoice over them, and make merry, and shall send gifts one to another; because these two prophets tormented them that dwelt on the earth.

11:11 After three and a half days the Spirit of Life from Elohim re-entered them. They rose to their feet - and a great terror fell upon certain who saw them!

KJV: And after three days and an half the Spirit of life from God entered into them, and they stood upon their feet; and great fear fell upon them which saw them.

11:12 And they (the two witnesses) heard a great voice from heaven saying, "Come up here!" And they rose up in a cloud unto heaven, and their enemies saw them.

KJV: And they heard a great voice from heaven saying unto them, Come up hither. And they ascended up to heaven in a cloud; and their enemies beheld them.

11:13 In that very hour there was a great earthquake - and a tenth part - the richest part of the city fell. Seven thousand people died - and a great fear fell upon the others* - and they gave praise to Elohim in heaven.

*Note: Of those remaining many would be the remnant of believers who gave praise - and others awed by the power of Yehovah who sought to praise Him and seek His mercy - for God does not want any to perish, but to repent and return to Him.

KJV: And the same hour was there a great earthquake, and the tenth part of the city fell, and in the earthquake were slain of men seven thousand: and the remnant were affrighted, and gave glory to the God of heaven.

11:14 The second woe is passed, and the third comes quickly!

KJV: The second woe is past; and, behold, the third woe cometh quickly.

11:15 Then the seventh angel blew his shofar, and great voices were heard in heaven, singing the music of creation, "The kingdoms of this world have returned to our Lord God by the hand of our Lord Yeshua, and he will reign forever and ever. Amen!"

KJV: And the seventh angel sounded; and there were great voices in heaven, saying, The kingdoms of this world are become the kingdoms of our Lord, and of his Christ; and he shall reign for ever and ever.

11:16 And the twenty-four elders - who sit before Yehovah - fell upon their faces from their chairs and worshiped Yehovah.

KJV: And the four and twenty elders, which sat before God on their seats, fell upon their faces, and worshipped God,

11:17 *They were* saying, "We praise You Yehovah, Lord of Hosts! You are the Almighty - Who is, Who was, and Who will be! - For surely by Your power and might You reign."

KJV: Saying, We give thee thanks, O Lord God Almighty, which art, and wast, and art to come; because thou hast taken to thee thy great power, and hast reigned.

11:18 *The time of* **the nations* is complete. Therefore the time of Your wrath and judgment of the dead has come - to give recompense to your servants, the holy prophets, and the righteous who revere You - and** *judge* **the great and the small - and destroy those who corrupted the earth.**

> *Note: Yeshua says, in Luke 21:24 *"Jerusalem will be trampled by the nations until the times of the Gentiles are fulfilled."*

KJV: And the nations were angry, and thy wrath is come, and the time of the dead, that they should be judged, and that thou shouldest give reward unto thy servants the prophets, and to the saints, and them that fear thy name, small and great; and shouldest destroy them which destroy the earth.

11:19 The Temple of Yehovah aka (House of prayer) was opened in heaven, and the Ark of the tablets of the Covenant* was revealed in His Temple - and coming *from it* **were thunder, lightning and great hailstones.**

> *Note: In Greek the *"Ark of the tablets of the Covenant"* was changed to the *"ark of testament."* The New Testament is called the *Brit Hadashah* (New Covenant) in Hebrew. The Greeks changed this *"New Covenant"* (Jer 31:31) to the *"New Testament,"* such as in Hebrew Matthew 26:28 - Yeshua says *"this is my blood of the* **New Covenant...**" The Greeks did not want to accept the Covenant of the Torah - considered *'dead legalism'* - they wanted Greek doctrines.

KJV: And the temple of God was opened in heaven, and there was seen in his temple the ark of his testament: and there were lightnings, and voices, and thunderings, and an earthquake, and great hail.

Chapter 12

12:1 A great sign appeared in the heavens; a woman clothed with the sun, and the moon beneath her feet and upon her head a crown of twelve stars.

KJV: And there appeared a great wonder in heaven; a woman clothed with the sun, and the moon under her feet, and upon her head a crown of twelve stars:

12:2 She was with child, crying out - afflicted with birth pains - that she might give birth.

KJV: And she being with child cried, travailing in birth, and pained to be delivered.

12:3 And there appeared another sign in heaven - behold, a great fiery dragon, having seven heads and ten horns, and on his heads were seven crowns.

KJV: And there appeared another wonder in heaven; and behold a great red dragon, having seven heads and ten horns, and seven crowns upon his heads.

12:4 His tail swept away a third of the stars of heaven and threw them to the earth. The dragon stood before the woman about to give birth - so that when she gave birth - he might devour her child (the body of Christ).*

> *Note: The Messiah was already crucified. He will return but he will not be reborn by woman. It is his followers, the faithful remnant, the body of Christ, who Satan wants to devour now - and in the future!

KJV: And his tail drew the third part of the stars of heaven, and did cast them to the earth: and the dragon stood before the woman which was ready to be delivered, for to devour her child as soon as it was born.

12:5 She gave birth to a male child - who is destined to rule all the nations with a sceptre of iron. Her child was caught up to Yehovah and to His throne.*

> *Note: Sometimes this seems to be a flashback of the Messiah's trials in order to set the stage for the prophecy. Other times it seems clearer that it is his Messianic church in which he resides that is caught up in heaven by their martyrdom for the sake of his name. They are destined to rule the nations and share the throne with the Messiah (see Revelation 2:26 and 3:21).

KJV: And she brought forth a man child, who was to rule all nations with a rod of iron: and her child was caught up unto God, and to his throne.

12:6 The woman fled into the wilderness, where she had a place prepared by Yehovah, so that there she can be nourished for one thousand two hundred and sixty days.

KJV: And the woman fled into the wilderness, where she hath a place prepared of God, that they should feed her there a thousand two hundred and threescore days.

12:7 Then a great war arose in heaven - Michael (the archangel) and his angels fighting against the dragon. And the dragon and his (fallen) angels fought back.

KJV: And there was war in heaven: Michael and his angels fought against the dragon; and the dragon fought and his angels.

12:8 But they did not prevail, and there was no longer any place for them in heaven.*

*Note: Satan, and his minions, still had access to heaven to contend with Yehovah over the souls of those on earth, see Job 1:6. Now this access will be denied forevermore.

KJV: And prevailed not; neither was their place found any more in heaven.

12:9 That great dragon was thrown down, the ancient serpent, who is called Satan - the deceiver of the whole world - was thrown down to the earth, and his angels were thrown down with him.

KJV: And the great dragon was cast out, that old serpent, called the Devil, and Satan, which deceiveth the whole world: he was cast out into the earth, and his angels were cast out with him.

12:10 I heard a great voice in the heavens that said, "Now we will see salvation and the mighty deeds of our Elohim and His Messiah - because he (Satan) has been cast out who was their adversary - who accuses the brethren day and night before our God."

KJV: And I heard a loud voice saying in heaven, Now is come salvation, and strength, and the kingdom of our God, and the power of his Christ: for the accuser of our brethren is cast down, which accused them before our God day and night.

12:11 They have conquered him (Satan) by the blood of the Lamb and by the Word of his Covenant* - for they loved not their lives even unto death.

*Note: The Greeks replaced the Hebrew word "covenant" with "testimony" or "testament," see Matthew 26:28 in the Hebrew, "This is my blood of the New Covenant shed for many for the remission of sin." Hebrew scribes acknowledge the Ark of the Testimony is the Ark of the Covenant, see Exodus 16:34. Some versions still use "testament" or "testimony" for "covenant" here and in other verses. For example, the New Covenant in Hebrew - Brit Hadashah - is called the New Testament in Greek.

KJV: And they overcame him by the blood of the Lamb, and by the word of their testimony; and they loved not their lives unto the death.

12:12 Therefore, rejoice O heavens and all who live in them! *But* **woe to those who dwell in the land and the sea - for Satan has come down to you with his great wrath - knowing that his time is short.**

KJV: Therefore rejoice, ye heavens, and ye that dwell in them. Woe to the inhabiters of the earth and of the sea! for the devil is come down unto you, having great wrath, because he knoweth that he hath but a short time.

12:13 When the dragon saw that he had been banished to the earth - he pursued the woman of Shiloh* - who had given birth to the male child (the body of Christ).

> *Note: This is a reference to Gen 49:10, *"The sceptre shall not depart from Judah… until Shiloh comes - and unto him will be the gathering of the people."* The gathering of the congregation is also associated with Shiloh in Joshua 18:1.

KJV: And when the dragon saw that he was cast unto the earth, he persecuted the woman which brought forth the man child.

12:14 The woman was given two wings of a great eagle* - so that she might fly into the wilderness - to a place chosen by Yehovah where she will be provided for a time, times, and a half a time, *away* **from the presence of the serpent.**

> *Note: This is a reference to Exodus 19:4, *"I bore you on eagle's wings and brought you unto Myself."* Also see Isaiah 40:31, *"They that wait upon Yehovah shall renew their strength, they shall mount up with wings as eagles - they shall run and not be weary, and they shall walk and not faint."*

KJV: And to the woman were given two wings of a great eagle, that she might fly into the wilderness, into her place, where she is nourished for a time, and times, and half a time, from the face of the serpent.

78

12:15 To silence her, the serpent poured water like a great flood out of his mouth - after the woman - to sweep her away.

KJV: And the serpent cast out of his mouth water as a flood after the woman, that he might cause her to be carried away of the flood.

12:16 The woman was delivered by the earth - which opened its mouth and swallowed the waters that the dragon had cast after her.

KJV: And the earth helped the woman, and the earth opened her mouth, and swallowed up the flood which the dragon cast out of his mouth.

12:17 The dragon became furious with the woman and went to make war with the remnant of her seed - those who keep the commandments of Yehovah and hold to the Covenant* of Yeshua the Messiah.

> *Note: The words for "covenant" and "testimony" (or "testament") are used interchangeably far too often in both our Greek and Hebrew manuscripts. In this context it means "covenant," see note in Rev. 12:11. A covenant is a contract, a solemn formalized promise, a testimony is not.

KJV: And the dragon was wroth with the woman, and went to make war with the remnant of her seed, which keep the commandments of God, and have the testimony of Jesus Christ.

Chapter 13

13:1 Then I stood upon the sand of the sea.   I saw a beast rising from the sea. It had seven heads and ten horns.   Upon its horns were ten crowns.   Upon its (seven) heads were blasphemous names of slander and mockery *of God!*

KJV: And I stood upon the sand of the sea, and saw a beast rise up out of the sea, having seven heads and ten horns, and upon his horns ten crowns, and upon his heads the name of blasphemy.

13:2 And the beast that I saw was like a leopard. His feet were like the feet of a bear. His mouth was like the mouth of a lion. The dragon gave the beast his power and great authority.

KJV: And the beast which I saw was like unto a leopard, and his feet were as the feet of a bear, and his mouth as the mouth of a lion: and the dragon gave him his power, and his seat, and great authority.

13:3 I saw one of its heads. It had been mortally wounded - but its deadly wound was healed. All the world marveled and followed the beast.

KJV: And I saw one of his heads as it were wounded to death; and his deadly wound was healed: and all the world wondered after the beast.

13:4 They worshiped the dragon who gave power to the beast.   They also worshiped the beast, saying, "Who is like the beast? Who is able to wage war with him?"

KJV: And they worshipped the dragon which gave power unto the beast: and they worshipped the beast, saying, Who is like unto the beast? who is able to make war with him?

13:5 It was given to it (the beast) to speak boastful words and blasphemies - and it was given power to act for forty-two months.

KJV: And there was given unto him a mouth speaking great things and blasphemies; and power was given unto him to continue forty two months.

13:6 She (the beast) opened her mouth in blasphemy against Yehovah, to blaspheme His Name and His tabernacle, and those who dwell in heaven.

KJV: And he opened his mouth in blasphemy against God, to blaspheme his name, and his tabernacle, and them that dwell in heaven.

13:7 Power was given to *the beast* to wage war with the saints and to overcome them. It was given power over every tribe and people and tongue and nation.

KJV: And it was given unto him to make war with the saints, and to overcome them: and power was given him over all kindreds, and tongues, and nations.

13:8 All the inhabitants of the earth are worshiping the beast. Everyone whose name was not written in the book of life of the Lamb who has been slain - *anointed* since the foundation of the world.

KJV: And all that dwell upon the earth shall worship him, whose names are not written in the book of life of the Lamb slain from the foundation of the world.

13:9 If anyone has ears - listen and heed!

KJV: If any man have an ear, let him hear.

13:10 Whoever has taken a prisoner - he will be taken prisoner. Likewise, he who kills by the sword - he will be killed by the sword. However, with the saints - there is hope and faith!

KJV: He that leadeth into captivity shall go into captivity: he that killeth with the sword must be killed with the sword. Here is the patience and the faith of the saints.

13:11 Then I saw another creature coming up out of the earth - and it had two horns like a lamb - and it spoke like a serpent.

> *Note: This may be a picture of the anti-Christ, appearing as a lamb, but speaking with the lies of the serpent, to convince those - who would normally recoil - to follow the beast.

KJV: And I beheld another beast coming up out of the earth; and he had two horns like a lamb, and he spake as a dragon.

13:12 It exercised all of the power of the first beast - and it caused all the earth and its inhabitants to worship the first beast - which was healed from the deadly wound.

KJV: And he exerciseth all the power of the first beast before him, and causeth the earth and them which dwell therein to worship the first beast, whose deadly wound was healed.

13:13 It will perform great signs, even making fire come down from heaven onto the earth in the sight of men.

KJV: And he doeth great wonders, so that he maketh fire come down from heaven on the earth in the Iof men,

13:14 It deceived the inhabitants of the earth by the performance of signs and wonders - that were permitted to be done by the beast - saying to the inhabitants of the earth - make an image of the beast *mortally* wounded by a sword who yet lived.

KJV: And deceiveth them that dwell on the earth by the means of those miracles which he had power to do in the sight of the beast; saying to them that dwell on the earth, that they should make an image to the beast, which had the wound by a sword, and did live.

13:15 It was given power to give breath to the image of the beast - that the image of the beast will speak and cause those to be killed - who would not worship the image of the beast.

KJV: And he had power to give life unto the image of the beast, that the image of the beast should both speak, and cause that as many as would not worship the image of the beast should be killed.

13:16 It will force everyone - the small and great, the rich and poor, the children of the free and the slaves - to receive a mark upon their hand, or forehead.

KJV: And he causeth all, both small and great, rich and poor, free and bond, to receive a mark in their right hand, or in their foreheads:

13:17 So that no one may buy or sell - except the one who has the mark of the beast - or the number of his name.

KJV: And that no man might buy or sell, save he that had the mark, or the name of the beast, or the number of his name.

13:18 Here is wisdom and understanding. Let one who is mindful calculate the number of the beast - for it is the number belonging to one man (Adam): His number is 666.

> Note: There is a lot to unpack here. Adam is the original man who was disobedient and rebellious. Adam passed his own image of disobedience on to all men (Gen 5:3). However, this beast is thought to be Lucifer, a fallen angel, also disobedient. So is 666 a man or beast or symbol? Regardless, disobedience to God is the original sin that defines mankind.

KJV: Here is wisdom. Let him that hath understanding count the number of the beast: for it is the number of a man; and his number is Six hundred threescore and six.

Chapter 14

14:1 I looked and behold! A Lamb (Yeshua) stood upon Mount Zion, and with him 144,000 upon whose foreheads is written the name of his Father (Yehovah).

KJV: And I looked, and, lo, a Lamb stood on the mount Sion, and with him an hundred forty and four thousand, having his Father's name written in their foreheads.

14:2 I heard a voice from heaven - like the voice of many waters - and like the sound of a great earthquake. The sound that I heard was much like the music of the stringed instruments which they were playing.

KJV: And I heard a voice from heaven, as the voice of many waters, and as the voice of a great thunder: and I heard the voice of harpers harping with their harps:

14:3 They sang a renewed song before the throne, and before the four *divine* living beings, and the elders, and certainly no one was able to learn the song, except the 144,000 who were purchased from the earth (with the blood of Yeshua).

KJV: And they sung as it were a new song before the throne, and before the four beasts, and the elders: and no man could learn that song but the hundred and forty and four thousand, which were redeemed from the earth.

14:4 These are those who were with women - but they were not defiled* - because they are still as virgins. These follow after the lamb everywhere that he goes. They are

people who have been redeemed* for Yehovah - and for the Lamb - they are the firstfruits.

> *Note: The often-used metaphor for worshiping other gods (or goddesses) is fornication or adultery. This is not about women themselves being a defilement (see Hebrews 13:4). Many cults in the first century were marked by revelry, drunkenness and licentious sexuality - so the metaphor is fitting. In desperate times they turned to human sacrifice of babies to appease their gods. These are the saints who have been bought by the blood of Yeshua. They are virgin in the sense they have never worshiped other gods or goddesses. They are devoted to the Lamb.

KJV: These are they which were not defiled with women; for they are virgins. These are they which follow the Lamb whithersoever he goeth. These were redeemed from among men, being the firstfruits unto God and to the Lamb.

14:5 In their mouths deception was not found, because they were blameless before the throne of Elohim.

KJV: And in their mouth was found no guile: for they are without fault before the throne of God.

14:6 I saw another angel flying in the midst of heaven - bringing the everlasting good news to declare to those who dwell upon the earth - for all the nations, tribes, tongues, and peoples.

KJV: And I saw another angel fly in the midst of heaven, having the everlasting gospel to preach unto them that dwell on the earth, and to every nation, and kindred, and tongue, and people,

14:7 Saying to them in a great voice: "Fear Elohim, and give him glory, because the hour of His judgment has come. And they worshiped Him Who made the heavens, and the earth, and the seas, and the springs.

KJV: Saying with a loud voice, Fear God, and give glory to him; for the hour of his judgment is come: and worship him that made heaven, and earth, and the sea, and the fountains of waters.

14:8 Another angel followed, saying, "She is fallen! She is fallen! Babylon the great - who made the whole earth *delirious* from her wine - which the nations drank - causing madness to fall upon the nations!"

KJV: And there followed another angel, saying, Babylon is fallen, is fallen, that great city, because she made all nations drink of the wine of the wrath of her fornication.

14:9 The third angel followed after them, saying in a great voice (that) if anyone worship the beast, and his image, and takes the mark in his forehead, or in his hand -

KJV: And the third angel followed them, saying with a loud voice, If any man worship the beast and his image, and receive his mark in his forehead, or in his hand,

14:10 - they will drink from the wine of the fierce wrath of Elohim, which is mixed in the cup of his wrath. He will mix it with troubles, fire, and brimstone, in the presence of the Lamb and his holy angels.

KJV: The same shall drink of the wine of the wrath of God, which is poured out without mixture into the cup of his indignation; and he shall be tormented with fire and brimstone in the presence of the holy angels, and in the presence of the Lamb:

14:11 The smoke of their torment will rise forever and ever - not one of them will have rest day or night, who worshiped the beast and its image - whoever took the mark of its name.

KJV: And the smoke of their torment ascendeth up for ever and ever: and they have no rest day nor night, who worship the beast and his image, and whosoever receiveth the mark of his name.

14:12 Here is found what the saints were waiting for - *those* who keep the commandments of Yehovah - and the faith of Yeshua.

KJV: Here is the patience of the saints: here are they that keep the commandments of God, and the faith of Jesus

14:13 I heard a divine voice from the heavens say to me, "Write! - blessed are those who die for the holiness of Yehovah - for the Spirit says those who live by their deeds - their deeds will follow them."

KJV: And I heard a voice from heaven saying unto me, Write, Blessed are the dead which die in the Lord from henceforth: Yea, saith the Spirit, that they may rest from their labours; and their works do follow them.

14:14 I looked and behold! There was a white cloud - upon the cloud someone sits like the Son of man - who has a golden crown upon his head - and a sharp sickle in his hand.

KJV: And I looked, and behold a white cloud, and upon the cloud one sat like unto the Son of man, having on his head a golden crown, and in his hand a sharp sickle.

14:15 Another angel came out of the temple - calling in a divine voice to he who sat on the cloud, "Send forth, please your sickle and reap - because the hour has come to reap - the harvest of the earth is ripe."

KJV: And another angel came out of the temple, crying with a loud voice to him that sat on the cloud, Thrust in thy sickle, and reap: for the time is come for thee to reap; for the harvest of the earth is ripe.

14:16 He who was sitting on the cloud sent forth his sickle to the earth - and the earth was reaped.

KJV: And he that sat on the cloud thrust in his sickle on the earth; and the earth was reaped.

14:17 Another angel appeared from the temple which was in heaven. He also had a sharp sickle.

KJV: And another angel came out of the temple which is in heaven, he also having a sharp sickle.

14:18 Yet another angel went out from the altar and he had authority over fire. With the sickle in his hand, he shouted with a loud voice, "Strike with your sickle and harvest the grapes of the earth, because her fruits have ripened!"

KJV: And another angel came out from the altar, which had power over fire; and cried with a loud cry to him that had the sharp sickle, saying, Thrust in thy sharp sickle, and gather the clusters of the vine of the earth; for her grapes are fully ripe.

14:19 The angel struck with his sickle and harvested the grapes of the earth and threw them in the great winepress of the wrath of Yehovah.

KJV: And the angel thrust in his sickle into the earth, and gathered the vine of the earth, and cast it into the great winepress of the wrath of God.

14:20 The winepress was trodden outside the city - and blood came out from the winepress up to the horses' bridles for a length of some 1600 furlongs.*

> *Note: The word used in Hebrew is תרבכ ארץ *kivrat eretz*, "a little distance of land." This Hebrew idiom is derived from horse racing.

KJV: And the winepress was trodden without the city, and blood came out of the winepress, even unto the horse bridles, by the space of a thousand and six hundred furlongs.

Chapter 15

15:1 I saw another sign in heaven, great and astonishing! Seven angels *were* coming and in their hands *were* the seven last plagues - the final wrath of Elohim - yet to be fulfilled!

KJV: And I saw another sign in heaven, great and marvellous, seven angels having the seven last plagues; for in them is filled up the wrath of God

15:2 I saw a vision, like unto a sea of crystal glass mixed with fire. They who overcame the beast and its idol - and the number of its name - *were* standing on the sea of crystal glass - holding the harps of Elohim -

KJV: And I saw, as it were a sea of glass mingled with fire: and them that had gotten the victory over the beast, and over his image, and over his mark, *and* over the number of his name, stand on the sea of glass, having the harps of God.

15:3 And (they were) singing the song of Moses, servant of Elohim - and the song of the Lamb, saying - "Great and marvelous are Your works - Yehovah, God of Hosts - Righteous and true are your ways, Oh King of kings!"

KJV: And they sing the song of Moses the servant of God, and the song of the Lamb, saying, Great and marvellous are thy works, Lord God Almighty; just and true are thy ways, thou King of saints.

15:4 " Who will not fear you, nor magnify Your Name, oh Elohim? Truly, You alone are righteous - all the nations will come and bow down before you - as your judgments are revealed!

KJV: Who shall not fear thee, O Lord, and glorify thy name? for thou only art holy: for all nations shall come and worship before thee; for thy judgments are made manifest.

15:5 After this - Behold! I saw the ark of the covenant* was opened in the heavens.

> *Note: See Revelation 11:19 on the reappearance of the Ark of the Covenant, and Jeremiah 3:16 which chronicles the disappearance of the Ark of the Covenant - apparently taken up by the end of Solomon's reign, who reintroduced sacrifice of babies to Moloch, an abomination to Yehovah.

KJV: After these things I looked, and behold, the temple of the tabernacle of the testimony in heaven was opened.

15:6 Seven angels appeared from the temple - who had the seven plagues - clothed in pure bright linen - their chests girded with golden belts.

KJV: And the seven angels came out of the temple, having the seven plagues, clothed in pure and white linen, and having their breasts girded with golden girdles.

15:7 One of the four *divine* living creatures gave unto the seven angels - seven golden bowls - full of the wrath of Yehovah - Who lives forever and ever.

KJV: And one of the four beasts gave unto the seven angels seven golden vials full of the wrath of God, who liveth for ever and ever.

15:8 The temple of God (house of prayer) was filled with the glory of Yehovah and His mighty power - no one will be able to enter the temple until the seven plagues of the seven angels are fulfilled!

KJV: And the temple was filled with smoke from the glory of God, and from his power; and no man was able to enter into the temple, till the seven plagues of the seven angels were fulfilled.

Chapter 16

16:1 I heard the great voice from heaven proclaiming to the seven angels, "Go, and pour out the seven cups of Yehovah's wrath on the earth!"

KJV: And I heard a great voice from heaven saying to seven angels go and pour out the seven cups of Elohim's judgment on the earth

16:2 The first angel went and poured out his bowl upon the earth - and a heavy plague came upon the earth. It was very, very bad for the people who had the mark of the beast on them - who prostrated themselves before the beast and its image.

KJV: And the first went, and poured out his vial upon the earth; and there fell a noisome and grievous sore upon the men which had the mark of the beast, and upon them which worshipped his image.

16:3 The second angel poured out his bowl into the sea - and it was changed into the blood of the dying - and every living creature *which it touched* died in the sea.

KJV: And the second angel poured out his vial upon the sea; and it became as the blood of a dead man: and every living soul died in the sea.

16:4 The third (angel) poured out his bowl into rivers and reservoirs of water, and the waters became blood.

KJV: And the third angel poured out his vial upon the rivers and fountains of waters; and they became blood.

16:5 I heard the angel of the waters saying, "You, Yehovah,

the Righteous One - Who was, Who is and Who will be - are holy and You have judged this."

KJV: And I heard the angel of the waters say, Thou art righteous, O Lord, which art, and wast, and shalt be, because thou hast judged thus.

16:6 Since they have shed the blood of saints and prophets - You have given them(deadly) blood to drink- for they deserve it!

KJV: For they have shed the blood of saints and prophets, and thou hast given them blood to drink; for they are worthy.

16:7 Then I heard a second (voice) saying, "Truly! Yehovah, God Almighty - Your judgments are righteous and true."

KJV: And I heard another out of the altar say, Even so, Lord God Almighty, true and righteous are thy judgments.

16:8 The fourth angel poured out his bowl into the sun - giving it power to afflict the world with great fire and destruction!

KJV: And the fourth angel poured out his vial upon the sun; and power was given unto him to scorch men with fire.

16:9 They (the unrepentant ones) blasphemed the name of Yehovah - Who has authority over these plagues and they did not return in repentance to give Him glory.

KJV: And men were scorched with great heat, and blasphemed the name of God, which hath power over these plagues: and they repented not to give him glory.

16:10 The fifth angel poured out his bowl upon the throne of the beast; and its kingdom became darkness. They gnawed their tongues from anguish and pain.

KJV: And the fifth angel poured out his vial upon the seat of the beast; and his kingdom was full of darkness; and they gnawed their tongues for pain

16:11   They cursed the God of the heavens because of their pain and wounds - but they did not turn back in repentance of their deeds.

KJV: And blasphemed the God of heaven because of their pains and their sores, and repented not of their deeds.

16:12 The sixth angel poured out his bowl into that great River Euphrates and dried up its waters to prepare the way for the kings from the east (sunrise).

> *Note: Right now, the Euphrates - once a great river - is indeed rapidly and completely drying up!

KJV: And the sixth angel poured out his vial upon the great river Euphrates; and the water thereof was dried up, that the way of the kings of the east might be prepared.

16:13 I saw, coming out from the mouth of the dragon, and from the mouth of the beast, and from the mouth of the prophet of deceit, three unclean spirits resembling reptiles!*

> *Note: The word in Hebrew means *"creeping things"* a reference to reptiles.

KJV: And I saw three unclean spirits like frogs come out of the mouth of the dragon, and out of the mouth of the beast, and out of the mouth of the false prophet.

16:14 They (the reptiles) are the spirits of demons, performing signs, and going out to the kings of all the earth to gather them for the war of the great day *against* God Almighty.

Note: Satan is gathering his armies from the leaders of all the nations of this world.

KJV: For they are the spirits of devils, working miracles, which go forth unto the kings of the earth and of the whole world, to gather them to the battle of that great day of God Almighty.

16:15 Behold, I come stealthily. Blessed is he who is vigilant and maintains his garments (armor) - who does not walk uncovered *so* they will not see his shame.*

*Note: Yeshua is gathering his spiritual warriors. They need to be alert, ready to go, prepared mentally, and spiritually cleansed for the battle ahead - dressed in their *'garments'* - the armor of God. To be unprepared when they are called to battle would be shameful and evident to all. He is doing this quietly, surreptitiously - the idiom used is *"like a thief"* - unnoticed and in secret.

KJV: Behold, I come as a thief. Blessed is he that watcheth, and keepeth his garments, lest he walk naked, and they see his shame.

16:16 He (Yehovah) will gather them in a place called (in Hebrew) "Armageddon.

Note: Almighty God is in charge - bringing the opponents together at a place of His choosing with Yeshua leading His forces into the final battle at Armageddon. The word in Hebrew can be construed as Mount Megedim (Har Megiddo).

KJV: And he gathered them together into a place called in the Hebrew tongue Armageddon.

16:17 Then the seventh angel poured out his bowl upon the wind - and there came a great voice out of the temple, from the throne, saying, "It is finished!"

KJV: And the seventh angel poured out his vial into the air; and there came a great voice out of the temple of heaven, from the throne, saying, It is done.

16:18 And there was *great* lightning and sounds of thunder - and huge earthquakes like have never happened since there were humans on the earth.

KJV: And there were voices, and thunders, and lightnings; and there was a great earthquake, such as was not since men were upon the earth, so mighty an earthquake, and so great.

16:19 The great city was split into three parts. The cities of the nations fell. Babylon the Great was judged before God to give unto her the bowl of His fierce wrath.

KJV: And the great city was divided into three parts, and the cities of the nations fell: and great Babylon came in remembrance before God, to give unto her the cup of the wine of the fierceness of his wrath.

16:20 Islands disappeared - and mountains (were levelled) - could no longer be found.

KJV: And every island fled away, and the mountains were not found.

16:21 Huge hailstones the weight of a talent* came down from heaven upon mankind. People cursed God because the death from the hailstones was very great!

> *Note: A *"talent"* is a weight of silver, 38 kilograms, which would make a deadly hailstone.

KJV: And there fell upon men a great hail out of heaven, every stone about the weight of a talent: and men blasphemed God because of the plague of the hail; for the plague thereof was exceeding great.

Chapter 17

17:1 There came one of the seven angels - who had one of the seven bowls - came and spoke with me, saying, "Come and I will show you the judgment of the great harlot who sits upon the many waters.

KJV: And there came one of the seven angels which had the seven vials, and talked with me, saying unto me, Come hither; I will shew unto thee the judgment of the great whore that sitteth upon many waters:

17:2 With her the kings of the earth have fornicated, and the inhabitants of the earth have become drunk with the wine of her fornication!"

KJV: With whom the kings of the earth have committed fornication, and the inhabitants of the earth have been made drunk with the wine of her fornication.

17:3 The hand of the Spirit brought me into the wilderness. I saw her - the one who sits on the scarlet beast - full of the reproach of her blasphemous names, having seven heads and ten horns.

KJV: So he carried me away in the spirit into the wilderness: and I saw a woman sit upon a scarlet coloured beast, full of names of blasphemy, having seven heads and ten horns.

17:4 The woman was dressed in scarlet and blue, and decked out with gold, precious stones, and pearls - having a golden cup in her hand full of abomination - full of the uncleanness of her fornication rites.

Note: Human sacrifice, drinking the blood of sacrifice, ritual fornication, and blasphemy are the mainstays of Satanic worship. Whatever is most offensive to God Almighty.

KJV: And the woman was arrayed in purple and scarlet colour, and decked with gold and precious stones and pearls, having a golden cup in her hand full of abominations and filthiness of her fornication:

17:5 On her forehead was written the name - Mystery Babylon the Great - the mother of harlots and abominations of the earth.

KJV: And upon her forehead was a name written, MYSTERY, BABYLON THE GREAT, THE MOTHER OF HARLOTS AND ABOMINATIONS OF THE EARTH.

17:6 And I saw a woman drunk from the blood of the saints - the blood of the martyrs for Yeshua! I was completely astonished at what I saw!

KJV: And I saw the woman drunken with the blood of the saints, and with the blood of the martyrs of Jesus: and when I saw her, I wondered with great admiration

17:7 The angel said to me, "Why are you *so* astonished? Behold, I will tell you the secret of the woman - and the beast which is carrying her - having seven heads and ten horns."

KJV: And the angel said unto me, Wherefore didst thou marvel? I will tell thee the mystery of the woman, and of the beast that carrieth her, which hath the seven heads and ten horns.

17:8 Behold, the beast* which you saw - was and is no more - and will come up from the abyss and go to Sheol. The inhabitants of the earth will be shocked - *those* whose names are not written in the Book of Life - from the beginning of the world - they see the beast that was and is no more.

> *Note: This is the Mystery - a supernatural beast who exists outside of our conception of time - from the beginning of the world - the pure bloody evil of the harlot and the beast will be sickeningly inconceivable to most.

KJV: The beast that thou sawest was, and is not; and shall ascend out of the bottomless pit, and she will go into perdition: and they that dwell on the earth shall wonder, whose names were not written in the book of life from the foundation of the world, when they behold the beast that was, and is not, and yet is.

17:9 "This is the meaning of wisdom. The seven heads, they are the seven mountains upon which the woman dwells - and which are the seven (fallen) angels."

KJV: And here is the mind which hath wisdom. The seven heads are seven mountains, on which the woman sitteth.

17:10 Also seven kings, five of them are fallen, and one still is and the other has not yet come. When he comes his time will be short.

> Note: The words for "angel" and "king" are all but identical - the only difference is one vowel. In texts without vowel markings, they are easily confused. The final battle is raging. Five have already been defeated. There are some left.

KJV: And there are seven kings: five are fallen, and one is, and the other is not yet come; and when he cometh, he must continue a short space.

17:11 The beast - which was, but is not - is the eighth (fallen angel), and is with the seven who go down to defeat and Sheol.

KJV: And the beast that was, and is not, even he is the eighth, and is of the seven, and goeth into perdition.

17:12 The ten horns that you saw - they are ten kings which have not yet received a kingdom - but they

received power as kings for one hour *to* rule along with the beast.

KJV: "And the ten horns which thou sawest are ten kings, which have received no kingdom as yet; but receive power as kings one hour with the beast."

17:13 To these (kings) was given one purpose - their forces shall be given *to* the beast.

KJV: These have one mind, and shall give their power and strength unto the beast.

17:14 They will make war with the Lamb - and the Lamb will prevail over them! For he is the Lord of Lords, and King of kings - and those with him are *his* chosen believers.

KJV: These shall make war with the Lamb, and the Lamb shall overcome them: for he is Lord of lords, and King of kings: and they that are with him are called, and chosen, and faithful.

17:15 And he said to me, "The waters which you saw there - where the harlot sits - they are the multitudes, and nations, and tongues.

KJV: And he saith unto me, The waters which thou sawest, where the whore sitteth, are peoples, and multitudes, and nations, and tongues.

17:16 The ten horns that you saw on the beast (the ten kings), they are haters of the whore - and they will betray her, and eat her flesh, and burn her with fire.

KJV: And the ten horns which thou sawest upon the beast, these shall hate the whore, and shall make her desolate and naked, and shall eat her flesh, and burn her with fire.

17:17 Because God has given into their hearts that they

will accomplish His will - and they will give the kingdom to the beast - until they fulfill the word of Elohim.

KJV: For God hath put in their hearts to fulfil his will, and to agree, and give their kingdom unto the beast, until the words of God shall be fulfilled.

17:18 The woman which you saw - she is the great city - which rules over all the kings of the earth.

KJV: And the woman which thou sawest is that great city, which reigneth over the kings of the earth.

Chapter 18

18:1 After these things I saw another angel coming down from heaven with great power, and great courage, and the earth was lit by his splendor.

KJV: And after these things I saw another angel come down from heaven, having great power; and the earth was lightened with his glory.

18:2 He proclaimed strongly, saying, "Fallen! Fallen! - is Babylon the great! And she has become a dwelling place of demons, along with every unclean spirit, guarded by *vultures*.*

> *Note: They are described as *"unclean and hated birds!"*

KJV: And he cried mightily with a strong voice, saying, Babylon the great is fallen, is fallen, and is become the habitation of devils, and the hold of every foul spirit, and a cage of every unclean and hateful bird,

18:3 All nations have drunk from the wine of her fornication! The kings of the earth have committed fornication with her - and by her power - merchants of the earth who lusted after her have become rich through her favors.

KJV: For all nations have drunk of the wine of the wrath of her fornication, and the kings of the earth have committed fornication with her, and the merchants of the earth are waxed rich through the abundance of her delicacies.

18:4 I heard another *divine* voice from heaven saying, "Depart from her! - So that you will not be partakers of her sins and receivers of her plagues."

Note: Even in Babylon there will be a faithful remnant. Yehovah is warning them to leave. Do not fall for her fate.

KJV: And I heard another voice from heaven, saying, Come out of her, my people, that ye be not partakers of her sins, and that ye receive not of her plagues.

18:5 For her sins have reached unto heaven - and Elohim has judged her iniquities.

KJV: For her sins have reached unto heaven, and God hath remembered her iniquities.

18:6 Give to her as she gave to you - double doubled according to her *evil* deeds - and in the cup she poured for you - you shall pour double for her.

KJV: Reward her even as she rewarded you, and double unto her double according to her works: in the cup which she hath filled fill to her double.

18:7 How she has glorified herself - and indulged herself! She has made her sins - *cause* your suffering. Rightly you will give her sorrow - to lament, and mourn - because she said in her heart - I will sit as queen - and I will never be a widow nor know lamentation.

KJV: How much she hath glorified herself, and lived deliciously, so much torment and sorrow give her: for she saith in her heart, I sit a queen, and am no widow, and shall see no sorrow.

18:8 Therefore in one day troubles, death, mourning, and famine will come to her - and she will be burnt by fire - because Elohim, who judges her - is Almighty!

KJV: Therefore shall her plagues come in one day, death, and mourning, and famine; and she shall be utterly burned with fire: for strong is the Lord God who judgeth her.

18:9 The kings of the earth wept and mourned over her - those who committed fornication with her and lived in self-indulgence - when they saw the smoke of her eternal burning!

KJV: And the kings of the earth, who have committed fornication and lived deliciously with her, shall bewail her, and lament for her, when they shall see the smoke of her burning,

18:10 *They are* standing afar - from fear of her torments - saying "Alas, Alas, for the great city Babylon - the mighty city - in one hour your judgment has come!"

KJV: Standing afar off for the fear of her torment, saying, Alas, alas, that great city Babylon, that mighty city! for in one hour is thy judgment come.

18:11 The merchants of the earth will weep and mourn for her - because no one will buy anymore:

KJV: And the merchants of the earth shall weep and mourn over her; for no man buyeth their merchandise any more:

18:12 the purchase of gold, and silver, and precious stones, and pearls, and fine linen, and purple and scarlet silk garments, and all manner of precious woods, and all vessels of ivory, and all jewelry of precious stones, and things of brass, and iron, and marble...

KJV: The merchandise of gold, and silver, and precious stones, and of pearls, and fine linen, and purple, and silk, and scarlet, and all thyine wood, and all manner vessels of ivory, and all manner vessels of most precious wood, and of brass, and iron, and marble,

18:13 and cinnamon and sweet perfumes, and ointments, and frankincense, and wine, and oil, and sifted fine flour, and wheat, and animals, and sheep, and horses, and chariots, and slaves, and the souls of men.

KJV: And cinnamon, and odours, and ointments, and frankincense, and wine, and oil, and fine flour, and wheat, and beasts, and sheep, and horses, and chariots, and slaves, and souls of men.

18:14 The fruit of the lust of your soul has come to an end, and all fat and precious things, they are lost from you and they can no longer be found.

> Note: There are many reasons why a wealthy trading city might lose its desirability for trade. Babylon was burning constantly possibly due to rioting and a total loss of law and order. No one wants to go in to the city to bring goods or to purchase them.

KJV: And the fruits that thy soul lusted after are departed from thee, and all things which were dainty and goodly are departed from thee, and thou shalt find them no more at all.

18:15 The merchants of these goods - which had made them rich - stood afar off from the fear of her torments - weeping, and mourning...

KJV: The merchants of these things, which were made rich by her, shall stand afar off for the fear of her torment, weeping and wailing

18:16 saying, "Woe, woe! To the city that was clothed in fine linen of crimson and blue - and was covered with gold and precious stones and pearls!"

KJV: And saying, Alas, alas, that great city, that was clothed in fine linen, and purple, and scarlet, and decked with gold, and precious stones, and pearls!

18:17 How many riches have been forsaken and lost in one hour! Every ruler, and every passing boat, and all ships and sailors of the sea - stood afar off!

KJV: For in one hour so great riches is come to nought. And every shipmaster, and all the company in ships, and sailors, and as many as trade by sea, stood afar off,

18:18 Crying out when they saw the city burning, saying of her, "What city has likened itself to this great city?"

KJV: And cried when they saw the smoke of her burning, saying, What city is like unto this great city!

18:19 They threw dust upon their heads, and they cried out, weeping and mourning, saying, "Woe, woe to her, the Great City - where they had enriched themselves from their trading - all of them who had ships in the sea - because she was destroyed in one hour!"

KJV: And they cast dust on their heads, and cried, weeping and wailing, saying, Alas, alas, that great city, wherein were made rich all that had ships in the sea by reason of her costliness! for in one hour is she made desolate

18:20 They exhorted one another over her - the saints and prophets - and rejoiced because Elohim had vindicated their judgments against her.

KJV: Rejoice over her, thou heaven, and ye holy apostles and prophets; for God hath avenged you on her.

18:21 An angel took a great stone, like a millstone, and threw it into the sea, saying, "With this *mighty* tempest you will cast out Babylon the great city - you will no longer find her."

KJV: And a mighty angel took up a stone like a great millstone, and cast it into the sea, saying, Thus with violence shall that great city Babylon be thrown down, and shall be found no more at all.

18:22 The sound of musicians, and singers and pipers, and those lifting the shofar, will no longer be heard in you at all - nor any craftsman or artist be found in you anymore' nor the grinding of a millstone (making flour) shall be heard anymore.

KJV: And the voice of harpers, and musicians, and of pipers, and trumpeters, shall be heard no more at all in thee; and no craftsman, of whatsoever craft he be, shall be found any more in thee; and the sound of a millstone shall be heard no more at all in thee;

18:23 The light of the candle will no longer shine in you, and you will no longer hear the voice of the bridegroom in you - because your merchants were the great powers of the earth - and with your sorceries you misled all the nations.

KJV: And the light of a candle shall shine no more at all in thee; and the voice of the bridegroom and of the bride shall be heard no more at all in thee: for thy merchants were the great men of the earth; for by thy sorceries were all nations deceived.

18:24 In her was found the blood of the prophets, and the saints, and everyone who was murdered upon the earth.

KJV: And in her was found the blood of prophets, and of saints, and of all that were slain upon the earth.

Chapter 19

19:1 After that I heard a voice like that of many trumpets in heaven saying, "Hallelujah! Glory and majesty and might be to Yehovah!"

KJV: And after these things I heard a great voice of many people in heaven, saying, Alleluia; Salvation, and glory, and honour, and power, unto the Lord our God:

19:2 His judgments are true and just - which He (Yehovah) judged against the whore (of Babylon) whose harlotry corrupted all the earth - and He took vengeance upon her who has on her hands the blood of His servants.

KJV: For true and righteous are his judgments: for he hath judged the great whore, which did corrupt the earth with her fornication, and hath avenged the blood of his servants at her hand.

19:3 They said once more: "HalleluYah!" - And the smoke rose up for ever and ever.

KJV: And again they said, Alleluia. And her smoke rose up for ever and ever.

19:4 So the twenty four elders and the four *divine living* creatures fell down and they worshiped Yehovah who sat upon the throne, saying "Hallelujah! Amen."

KJV: And the four and twenty elders and the four beasts fell down and worshiped God that sat on the throne, saying, Amen; Alleluia.

19:5 A voice went out from the throne, and said, "Praise

Yah, my servants! Praise Yehovah! Praise the name of Yehovah!" - And all the small and great before Him, feared his wrath!"

KJV: And a voice came out of the throne, saying, Praise our God, all ye his servants, and ye that fear him, both small and great.

19:6 I heard the sound of a large multitude - like the sound of many waters - it was like many voices saying, "Halleluyah Yehovah! For the Lord our God, the Almighty is king!"

KJV: And I heard as it were the voice of a great multitude, and as the voice of many waters, and as the voice of mighty thunderings, saying, Alleluia: for the Lord God omnipotent reigneth.

19:7 "Rejoice and be glad - and give him honor - for the time of the wedding of the Lamb has come and his bride has prepared herself."

KJV: Let us be glad and rejoice, and give honour to him: for the marriage of the Lamb is come, and his wife hath made herself ready.

19:8 And she (the bride) was given to clothe herself in pure white silk* - because it proclaims the righteousness of the saints - and she becomes beautiful.

> *Note: It says *silk* in the Gaster Hebrew manuscript. Silk מֶשִׁי (and linen) are also mentioned in Ezekiel 16:10 & 13 in the dressing of Israel. In the Freiberg Hebrew manuscript, it is *linen* בֻּוץ.

KJV: And to her was granted that she should be arrayed in fine linen, clean and white: for the fine linen is the righteousness of saints.

19:9 He (the angel) said to me - it is written, "Blessed are those who are called to the marriage supper of the Lamb." - "Truly these are the words of Elohim!"

KJV: And he saith unto me, Write, Blessed are they which are called unto the marriage supper of the Lamb. And he saith unto me, These are the true sayings of God.

19:10 I fell at his feet to bow down to him, and he said to me, "Do not bow down to me - for I serve together with you and the faithful - their testimony of Yeshua *came from* Yehovah - because the testimony of Yeshua is the spirit of prophecy."

KJV: And I fell at his feet to worship him. And he said unto me, See thou do it not: I am thy fellow servant, and of thy brethren that have the testimony of Jesus: worship God: for the testimony of Jesus is the spirit of prophecy.

19:11 I saw the heavens open, and beheld a white horse - and he who sat on it was called Faithful and True. He will conquer and judge in righteousness.

KJV: And I saw heaven opened, and behold a white horse; and he that sat upon him was called Faithful and True, and in righteousness he doth judge and make war.

19:12 His eyes are like a flame of fire - and on his head are many crowns - and he has a name written which he alone knows.

KJV: His eyes were as a flame of fire, and on his head were many crowns; and he had a name written, that no man knew, but he himself.

19:13 His clothing will be stained with blood - His name will be called the Word of God.

KJV: And he was clothed with a vesture dipped in blood: and his name is called The Word of God.

19:14 All the hosts of heaven, clothed in pure white silk*, follow him on white horses.

> *Note: The Freiberg Hebrew manuscript says, *"And the armies of heaven - which followed him on white horses - were clothed in pure white linen."* The Gaster Hebrew manuscript says *silk*.

KJV: And the armies which were in heaven followed him upon white horses, clothed in fine linen, white and clean.

19:15 From his mouth came a two-edged sword to smite the nations - he will reign over them with a sceptre of iron. He treads the winepress* of the wrath of Yehovah - Almighty God.

> *Note: Authority is given to Yeshua to judge and punish - in righteousness - all those evil ones who have aroused the anger of Yehovah - referred to here as the wine of the grapes of wrath.

KJV: And out of his mouth goeth a sharp sword, that with it he should smite the nations: and he shall rule them with a rod of iron: and he treadeth the winepress of the fierceness and wrath of Almighty God.

19:16 And a name *is* written upon His clothing, "King of Kings, and Lord of Lords."

KJV: And he hath on his vesture and on his thigh a name written, KING OF KINGS, AND LORD OF LORDS.

19:17 I saw an angel standing in the sun - calling with a loud voice - saying to all the *carrion** birds that fly in the heavens, "Come and gather for the great supper of God!"

> *Note:The text is referring to vultures preying upon the corpses.

KJV: And I saw an angel standing in the sun; and he cried with a loud voice, saying to all the fowls that fly in the midst of heaven, Come and gather yourselves together unto the supper of the great God;

19:18 And you (vultures) shall eat the flesh of kings - and the flesh of princes - and the flesh of mighty men *of*

war - and the flesh of horses - and the flesh of those who ride on them - and the flesh of the sons of nobles - *both* **the great and the small.**

KJV: That ye may eat the flesh of kings, and the flesh of captains, and the flesh of mighty men, and the flesh of horses, and of them that sit on them, and the flesh of all men, both free and bond, both small and great.

19:19 I saw the beast and the kings of the earth and their armies gathered to make war with him (Yeshua) who sat on the *white* **horse - and to fight with his army.**

KJV: And I saw the beast, and the kings of the earth, and their armies, gathered together to make war against him that sat on the horse, and against his army.

19:20 The beast and the false prophet were captured while performing miraculous signs - in order to incite those who took the mark of the beast. Those worshiping him (the beast) are *then* **cast alive into Sheol - the lake of fire burning with brimstone.**

KJV: And the beast was taken, and with him the false prophet that wrought miracles before him, with which he deceived them that had received the mark of the beast, and them that worshipped his image. These both were cast alive into a lake of fire burning with brimstone

19:21 The rest were killed by the sword of the Word *of God* **- that comes out of his mouth - who sits on the** *white* **horse - and all the beasts of the field feasted upon their flesh.**

KJV: And the remnant were slain with the sword of him that sat upon the horse, which sword proceeded out of his mouth: and all the fowls were filled with their flesh.

Chapter 20

20:1 I saw an angel coming down from heaven - having the key to the abyss in his hand - and a great chain.

KJV: And I saw an angel come down from heaven, having the key of the bottomless pit and a great chain in his hand.

20:2 And he (the angel) took hold of the dragon - the serpent of ancient times - who is the adversary (Satan) and bound him for a thousand years.

KJV: And he laid hold on the dragon, that old serpent, which is the Devil, and Satan, and bound him a thousand years,

20:3 He sent *Satan* into the abyss *to be* imprisoned - and (the angel) sealed *it* over him (Satan) so that he will no longer deceive the nations - until a thousand years have been completed - after which he will be released for a time.

KJV: And cast him into the bottomless pit, and shut him up, and set a seal upon him, that he should deceive the nations no more, till the thousand years should be fulfilled: and after that he must be loosed a little season.

20:4 I saw thrones, and those sitting upon them who were authorized to judge - those testifying of Yeshua and the Word of God. These are the ones who were slain - who did not take the mark of the beast upon their foreheads or their hands - nor did they worship the beast or his idol. They will live and rule the people with Yeshua for a thousand years.

KJV: And I saw thrones, and they sat upon them, and judgment was given unto them: and I saw the souls of them that were beheaded for the witness of Jesus, and for the word of God, and which had not worshipped the beast, neither his image, neither had received his mark upon their foreheads, or in their hands; and they lived and reigned with Christ a thousand years.

20:5 However, the rest of the dead do not arise until the thousand years are completed. This is the first resurrection.

KJV: But the rest of the dead lived not again until the thousand years were finished. This is the first resurrection.

20:6 Blessed is he who was set-apart by the first resurrection - for these there will be no second death - Only they shall be priests of Elohim and his Messiah - reigning *with them* for a thousand years.

KJV: Blessed and holy is he that hath part in the first resurrection: on such the second death hath no power, but they shall be priests of God and of Christ, and shall reign with him a thousand years.

20:7 After a thousand years the adversary (Satan) will be released from his prison.

KJV: And when the thousand years are expired, Satan shall be loosed out of his prison,

20:8 And he (Satan) shall go and entice the peoples throughout the four corners of the earth, and Gog and Magog, to gather his army for battle - for their number is as the sand of the sea.

KJV: And shall go out to deceive the nations which are in the four quarters of the earth, Gog, and Magog, to gather them together to battle: the number of whom is as the sand of the sea.

20:9 And they went up over the breadth of the earth, and encircled the tents of the saints, and the beloved holy city was filled with fire - and the fire of God came down from heaven and engulfed them (the army of Satan)!

KJV: And they went up on the breadth of the earth, and compassed the camp of the saints about, and the beloved city: and fire came down from God out of heaven, and devoured them.

20:10 Satan will be cast into the lake of fire and brimstone - where *along with* the beast and the false prophet *they* will suffer -day and night - for ever and ever!

KJV: And the devil that deceived them was cast into the lake of fire and brimstone, where the beast and the false prophet are, and shall be tormented day and night for ever and ever.

20:11 Then I saw a great, bright throne, and *the* One sitting on it was He from whom *the entities* of* the earth and the heavens fled - and they found no place for themselves.

> *Note: The evil-doers of the earth are fleeing before the wrath of God and finding no safe haven. These verses are a reference to 2nd Peter 3:10-13, *"the day of God. wherein the heavens being on fire shall be dissolved, and the elements shall melt with fervent heat... Nevertheless, we, according to His promise, look for new heavens and a new earth wherein dwells righteousness!"* The spiritual dimension creates the physical dimension. Satan and his fallen angels and beasts are not immortal but clearly a total house-cleaning of celestial wrath and heat will be required to dissolve those supernatural entities.

KJV: And I saw a great white throne, and him that sat on it, from whose face the earth and the heaven fled away; and there was found no place for them.

20:12 I saw the dead, both the least and great, standing before Elohim - and books were opened. Yet another

book was opened - this book was the Book of Life - to judge the dead according to that which was written in the books - according to their deeds.

KJV: And I saw the dead, small and great, stand before God; and the books were opened: and another book was opened, which is the book of life: and the dead were judged out of those things which were written in the books, according to their works.

20:13 Then the sea gave up the dead that were in it. Sheol also gave up its dead who were in it - each one of them will be judged according to their deeds.

KJV: And the sea gave up the dead which were in it; and death and hell delivered up the dead which were in them: and they were judged every man according to their works.

20:14 Then Death and Gehinnom (Hell itself) will be thrown into the fire: for this is the second death.

> Note: The physical body is the first death - then one is judged - and the spirit is the second death. But after this, God will destroy even Death itself and the fire of brimstone as well.

KJV: And death and hell were cast into the lake of fire. This is the second death.

20:15 Whoever is not found written in the Book of Life - will be thrown into the fire.

KJV: And whosoever was not found written in the book of life was cast into the lake of fire.

Chapter 21

21:1 I saw a new heaven and a new earth because the first heaven and the first earth have passed away and the sea is no more.

> Note: We referred previously (Rev 20:11) to 2nd Peter 3:10-13, *"We, according to His promise, look for new heavens and a new earth wherein dwells righteousness!"* God is doing a complete make-over.

KJV: And I saw a new heaven and a new earth: for the first heaven and the first earth were passed away; and there was no more sea.

21:2 Then I, John (Yohanan), saw the city of the Holy One, New Jerusalem, descending from God in heaven - having been made ready as a bride adorned for her husband.

KJV: And I John saw the holy city, new Jerusalem, coming down from God out of heaven, prepared as a bride adorned for her husband.

21:3 I heard a great voice from the throne saying, "Behold, the Tabernacle of Yehovah is among men - and He will dwell with them - and He shall be their God - and they shall be His people.

> Note: The Covenant from Exodus 34;10, is being renewed as in Jeremiah 31:31 and 32:36-38, also Matthew 26:28, *"This is my blood of the Renewed Covenant."* The Hebrew word *'hadashah'* means either *'new'* or *'renewed'* depending upon the context. You decide.

KJV: And I heard a great voice out of heaven saying, Behold, the tabernacle of God is with men, and he will dwell with them, and they shall be his people, and God himself shall be with them, and be their God.

21:4 Then Yehovah Elohim wiped away the tears from their faces - and there shall be no more death - nor mourning, nor crying, nor pain - there shall be no more - as the former things have passed away.

KJV: And God shall wipe away all tears from their eyes; and there shall be no more death, neither sorrow, nor crying, neither shall there be any more pain: for the former things are passed away.

21:5 And now, he who sits upon the throne says, "Behold, I make everything new!" - and He said to me "Write - for these words are very, very faithful and true!"

KJV: And he that sat upon the throne said, Behold, I make all things new. And he said unto me, Write: for these words are true and faithful.

21:6 He said to me, "It is finished. *I am the Aleph and the Tav* - the First and the Last - the Beginning and the End - I will freely give living water to those who thirst.

KJV: And he said unto me, It is done. I am Alpha and Omega, the beginning and the end. I will give unto him that is athirst of the fountain of the water of life freely.

21:7 He who prevails will inherit everything. I will be Elohim to him and he will be a son to me.

KJV: He that overcometh shall inherit all things; and I will be his God, and he shall be my son.

21:8 However, to the unbelievers, the murderers, the adulterers, the sorcerers, the deceivers - and to all the wicked - I will give a wage of fire from Sheol - the lake which burns by fire and brimstone. This is the second death!

KJV: But the fearful, and unbelieving, and the abominable, and murderers, and whoremongers, and sorcerers, and idolaters, and all liars, shall have their part in the lake which burneth with fire and brimstone: which is the second death.

117

21:9 One of the seven angels came to me - who had in their hands - the bowls which were filled with the seven last plagues - came to me and said, "Come and see the woman, the bride of the Lamb!"

KJV: And there came unto me one of the seven angels which had the seven vials full of the seven last plagues, and talked with me, saying, Come hither, I will shew thee the bride, the Lamb's wife.

21:10 And he carried me in the spirit to a great and lofty mountain and showed me the holy city of Jerusalem coming down from God in heaven.

KJV: And he carried me away in the spirit to a great and high mountain, and shewed me that great city, the holy Jerusalem, descending out of heaven from God,

21:11 The glory of Yehovah was upon her - and His light was like that of a precious stone called *emerald* - *which is* clear as crystal.

> Note: The KJV says *"jasper"* here - but the Greek word for jasper also has the meaning *"emerald"* which is more consistent to previous verses in Exodus 24:10 and Revelation 4:3. Because of their green color, clearness and brilliance, *"jasper," "emerald"* or *"sapphire"* appear to be used interchangeably.

KJV: Having the glory of God: and her light was like unto a stone most precious, even like a jasper stone, clear as crystal;

21:12 It (the holy city) shall have a great and high wall - which shall have twelve gates, and at the gates twelve angels - and written names - which shall be the names of the twelve tribes of the children of Israel.

KJV: And had a wall great and high, and had twelve gates, and at the gates twelve angels, and names written thereon, which are the names of the twelve tribes of the children of Israel:

21:13 From the east three gates and from the north three gates and from the south (Yemen) three gates and from the west three gates.

KJV: On the east three gates; on the north three gates; on the south three gates; and on the west three gates.

21:14 The wall of the city had twelve foundations - and in them were the names of the twelve sent ones of the Lamb.

> Note: The *"sent ones"* are messengers from God, in this case that could mean the twelve angel messengers to the churches mentioned earlier - or the twelve Apostles, who are not mentioned by name in Revelation except for John.

KJV: And the wall of the city had twelve foundations, and in them the names of the twelve apostles of the Lamb.

21:15 He that spoke with me had in his hand a golden reed to measure the city and its gates and wall.

> Note: This is another reference to the *"golden reed"* measuring rod from Ezekiel's vision chapter 40:3, and Revelation 11:1.

KJV: And he that talked with me had a golden reed to measure the city, and the gates thereof, and the wall thereof.

21:16 The city shall be square, and its length shall be like a square, and the city shall be measured with the golden reed - and the length and height and width shall be equal.

> Note: Although the text says *"like a square"* later it is measured in cubits in three dimensions so it may be better translated as a *"cube."*

KJV: And the city lieth foursquare, and the length is as large as the breadth: and he measured the city with the reed, twelve thousand furlongs. The length and the breadth and the height of it are equal.

21:17 Its wall measured one hundred and forty-four cubits according to man's measure *and that of* the angel.

> Note: It seems the man's measure is used by the angel so the man can understand it.

KJV: And he measured the wall thereof, an hundred and forty and four cubits, according to the measure of a man, that is, of the angel.

21:18 And the building of its wall was of jasper stone, but the city will be pure gold.

KJV: And the building of the wall of it was of jasper: and the city was pure gold, like unto clear glass.

21:19 The foundation of the wall and the city were adorned with fine stones - the first foundation was jasper, and the second one sapphire, and the third, chalcedon, and the fourth turquoise -

KJV: And the foundations of the wall of the city were garnished with all manner of precious stones. The first foundation was jasper; the second, sapphire; the third, a chalcedony; the fourth, an emerald;

21:20 - The fifth (foundation) was of ruby, the sixth of onyx, the seventh of chrysolite, the eighth of beryl, the ninth of topaz, the tenth of agate, the eleventh of jacinth (or ligure), and the twelfth was called - in a foreign tongue - *amethyst*.

> Note: None of the manuscripts, Hebrew or Greek, match in their descriptions or order of the stones, nor do they match precisely with the stones of the priestly garment, the Ephod in Exodus 28:17-20 which are the signet stones of the names of the twelve children of Israel.

KJV: The fifth, sardonyx; the sixth, sardius; the seventh, chrysolyte; the eighth, beryl; the ninth, a topaz; the tenth, a chrysoprasus; the eleventh, a jacinth; the twelfth, an amethyst.

21:21 The twelve gates shall be twelve pearls - each and every one are pearls - The streets of the city shall be pure gold like clear crystal.

> Note: *"Clear like crystal"* seems to be an idiomatic usage depicting purity and brilliance.

KJV: And the twelve gates were twelve pearls: every several gate was of one pearl: and the street of the city was pure gold, as it were transparent glass.

21:22 I saw no Temple in it - because Yehovah God Almighty and the Lamb - will be His Temple.

KJV: And I saw no temple therein: for the Lord God Almighty and the Lamb are the temple of it.

21:23 And the city needs no light from the sun or moon - because the glory of God and the Lamb will shine upon it.

KJV: And the city had no need of the sun, neither of the moon, to shine in it: for the glory of God did lighten it, and the Lamb is the light thereof.

21:24 For the blessed ones will walk in the light thereof - and the kings of the earth will bring their wealth into it.

KJV: And the nations of them which are saved shall walk in the light of it: and the kings of the earth do bring their glory and honour into it.

21:25 The gates will not be closed - because there will be no night there.

KJV: And the gates of it shall not be shut at all by day: for there shall be no night there.

21:26 And they (of the holy city) will bring greatness and splendor to all the nations.

KJV: And they shall bring the glory and honour of the nations into it.

21:27 And there shall not come in it anything that is defiled or that commits an abomination or deceit - only those written in the Book of Life.

KJV: And there shall in no wise enter into it any thing that defileth, neither whatsoever worketh abomination, or maketh a lie: but they which are written in the Lamb's book of life.

Chapter 22

22:1 The angel showed me the river of living water - pure as amethyst - going forth from the throne of God and the Lamb (in the holy city).

> Note: The metaphor of comparison to rare stones is omnipresent in Revelation. They are always used in description of Yehovah or something coming from Him. It expresses powerful beauty, light, purity, clarity and great value. The precious stones used most often are emerald, sapphire, jasper and amethyst.

KJV: And he shewed me a pure river of water of life, clear as crystal, proceeding out of the throne of God and of the Lamb.

22:2 In the midst of its way, here and there, by the river (of living water) will be the tree of life that yields twelve types of fruit - each for its month. Its fruit is for food - and its leaves are medicine for the healing of the nations.

KJV: And in the midst of the street of it, and on either side of the river, was there the tree of life, which bare twelve manner of fruits, and yielded her fruit every month: and the leaves of the tree were for the healing of the nations.

22:3 The cursing and destruction will be no more! The throne of Elohim and of the Lamb will be there (in the holy city) and His servants will serve Him.

KJV: And there shall be no more curse: but the throne of God and of the Lamb shall be in it; and his servants shall serve him:

22:4 His servants will see His face and His name will be written on their foreheads!

KJV: And they shall see his face; and his name shall be in their foreheads.

22:5 There will be no night - neither will they need the light of the sun or moon - for Yehovah will enlighten them - and they will reign (beside Him) forever and ever!

KJV: And there shall be no night there; and they need no candle, neither light of the sun; for the Lord God giveth them light: and they shall reign for ever and ever.

22:6 Then the angel said to me, "These words are absolutely faithful and true - and Yehovah - the God of the spirits of the prophets* - sent His angel to show His servants that which must be done quickly."

> Note: Many think of Revelation as standing apart and alone as a prophecy - but it is not. God here is validating all the prophets who spoke of the end times and whose words are quoted in the Book of Revelation, including Moses from Exodus, Isaiah, Jeremiah, Ezekiel, Micah, Zepheniah, Matthew, Peter, and Paul etcetera.

KJV: And he said unto me, These sayings are faithful and true: and the Lord God of the holy prophets sent his angel to shew unto his servants the things which must shortly be done.

22:7 "Behold! I (Yeshua) come quickly - blessed is the one who keeps the words of the prophecy of this book."

KJV: Behold, I come quickly: blessed is he that keepeth the sayings of the prophecy of this book.

22:8 And I, (John) Yohanan, heard and saw these things - and after I saw and heard - I fell down to bow at his feet (the angel) who showed me these things.

KJV: And I John saw these things, and heard them. And when I had heard and seen, I fell down to worship before the feet of the angel which shewed me these things.

22:9 And the angel said to me, "Do not do this! I too serve with you, and your brothers - the prophets - and those who keep the words of this prophecy. Pray to Yehovah!"

KJV: Then saith he unto me, See thou do it not: for I am thy fellowservant, and of thy brethren the prophets, and of them which keep the sayings of this book: worship God.

22:10 The angel said to me, "Do not seal the prophetic vision of this book - because the time is near!"

KJV: And he saith unto me, Seal not the sayings of the prophecy of this book: for the time is at hand.

22:11 Whoever is wicked shall be so for all time. Certainly, whoever is impure, will also be the same *for all time*. However, whoever is righteous will be so for all the time. And whoever is blessed shall continue to be so."

KJV: He that is unjust, let him be unjust still: and he which is filthy, let him be filthy still: and he that is righteous, let him be righteous still: and he that is holy, let him be holy still.

22:12 Behold! I come quickly and my reward is with me - to give to each and every one according to their deeds!

KJV: And, behold, I come quickly; and my reward is with me, to give every man according as his work shall be.

22:13 I am *the Alef and the Tav* - the First and the Last - the Beginning and the End!

KJV: I am Alpha and Omega, the beginning and the end, the first and the last.

22:14 Blessed are they who have washed their garments in the blood of the Lamb - They shall have the right *to eat of* the Tree of Life - They shall enter the gates of the *holy* city.

KJV: Blessed are they that do his commandments, that they may have right to the tree of life, and may enter in through the gates into the city.

22:15 Those outside - they are dogs, sorcerers, wicked ones, murderers, idolaters, prostitutes and liars.

KJV: For without are dogs, and sorcerers, and whoremongers, and murderers, and idolaters, and whosoever loveth and maketh a lie.

22:16 I, Yeshua, sent my angel to testify to you these things in the assemblies - for I am the root and seed of David - the bright morning star.

> Note: As I received from my Father - *"I (Yeshua) will give him the morning star."* (Revelation 2:28)

KJV: I Jesus have sent mine angel to testify unto you these things in the churches. I am the root and the offspring of David, and the bright and morning star.

22:17 For the Spirit and the bride say, "Please come, and he who hears will say come, and he who is thirsty will come, and he will drink of the priceless living water freely."

KJV: And the Spirit and the bride say, Come. And let him that heareth say, Come. And let him that is athirst come. And whosoever will, let him take the water of life freely.

22:18 I (the angel) testify to all who hear the words of the prophecy of this book: "If anyone adds certain words to it! Elohim will also add to him the plagues written in this book."*

> *Note: Woe to those who have manipulated this text by changing or inserting certain words that change or manipulate or take away from the meaning of the Word of God!

KJV: For I testify unto every man that heareth the words of the

126

prophecy of this book, If any man shall add unto these things, God shall add unto him the plagues that are written in this book:

22:19 If anyone belittles the words of God's prophecy - Elohim will remove his name and inheritance from the book of life - and the holy city - and the *blessings** written in this book.

> *Note: The Hebrew word used here מִירָבְד means *things, matters, issues, or words* - *"things"* in this context must refer to the *blessings,* such as eternal life.

KJV: And if any man shall take away from the words of the book of this prophecy, God shall take away his part out of the book of life, and out of the holy city, and from the things which are written in this book.

22:20 He who testifies to these things also said, "I (Yeshua) will come quickly!" Amen! come, Lord Yeshua.

KJV: He which testifieth these things saith, Surely I come quickly. Amen. Even so, come, Lord Jesus.

22:21 "The grace of our Lord Yeshua, the Messiah, be with you all, Amen!"

KJV: The grace of our Lord Jesus Christ be with you all. Amen.

The Hebrew Book of Revelation

Hebrew to English without Notes or KJV

Chapter 1

[1] The Revelation of Yeshua the Messiah, which Yehovah gave to him (John - Yohanan in Hebrew), to reveal to his servants the things that they must do at the time of the harvest.

[2] Elohim gave notice by his servant, John (Yochanan), who delivered the Word of Yehovah, along with the testimony of Yeshua the Messiah, about all that he saw.

[3] Blessed is the one who hears and proclaims the words of this prophecy and keeps what is written in it - for the time is near.

[4] I, John, who preceded the seven assemblies of Asia (Minor); grace and peace to you, from He - Who is, Who was, and Who will be - and from the seven spirits who stand before His throne.

[5] And from Yeshua the Messiah who is a faithful witness, the firstborn of the dead (saints), Head of kings of the earth - he who also loved us and washed us from our sins with his blood.

[6] Yeshua made us a kingdom of priests unto Yehovah, his Father. To Him is the glory and dominion forever and for all time to come. Amen!

[7] Behold, Yeshua shall come in the cloud (with rejoicing). Every eye will see him. All who hurt him will mourn because of him. And so, all families of the earth will also. Amen!

[8] I am the Aleph and the Tav, the First and the Last, says Yehovah Elohim - Who is, Who was, and Who will be - the Almighty.

[9] I am John - your brother - who shares in tribulation

with you, and who shares in the kingdom, and who awaits upon Yeshua the Messiah. I was on the island, which is named Patmos, in the presence of the Word of Yehovah through the illumination of Yeshua.

[10] Behold the Spirit soaked me at the beginning of the Sabbath, and I heard a great voice behind me like the voice of the trumpet.

[11] The voice said to me; What you see, write in a book, and send it to the seven assemblies which are in Asia (Minor) - Ephesus, and Smyrna, and Pergamus and Thyatira and Sardis and Philadelphia and Laodicea!

[12] Behold, I turned to see the voice that was speaking with me, and from the moment I turned, behold I saw seven golden Menorahs.

[13] In the midst of the seven golden Menorahs, I saw someone like unto the Son of Adam (Man) who is dressed in a garment reaching down to his feet, girded about his chest with a golden sash.

[14] His head and his hair are white as wool, white like snow, and his eyes resemble a flame of fire.

[15] His feet are like bronze from a fiery furnace, and his voice is like the sound of many waters.

[16] In his right hand were seven stars, and from his mouth went forth a two-edged sword, and his face resembled the shining light of the sun in its strength.

[17] When I saw him, I fell at his feet as if dead. He laid his right hand upon me, saying, Do not fear, I am the First and the Last.

[18] I am he who lives - but I was dead - and I was resurrected forever and ever. I have the keys of death and of Sheol.

[19] In truth, write what you saw, and what is now, and what will be after this.

[20] This is the secret of the seven stars which you saw in my right hand, and the seven golden Menorahs. They are the seven messengers of the assemblies, and the seven Menorahs indicate the seven assemblies.

Chapter 2

¹ Write to the messenger of the assembly in Ephesus: Behold! He who holds the seven stars which are in his right hand - he who walks in the midst of the seven golden Menorahs - it is he who says these things:

²˙How well I know your works and struggles, and your long suffering. I know that you do not tolerate evil people. You tested those that say they are apostles, but are not, and you found them liars!

3 You sacrificed and suffered for the sake of my name (Yeshua) yet you did not fall from faith.

⁴ Nevertheless, in any case, I do have matters to bring against you because you have abandoned your first love (Torah).

⁵ Therefore, remember your roots from which you have grown away. Repent and return to your first works! If not, behold, I will come to you in haste, and I will remove your Menorah from its place, if you will not repent.

⁶ But you still have this; that you hated the pagan works of the Nicolaitans, which I also abhorred.

⁷ Whoever has ears, let him hear what the Spirit says to the assemblies. Whoever overcomes - I will give to eat from the Tree of Life - which is in the Garden of Eden of my Elohim.

⁸ To the messenger of the assembly of Smyrna, write: Behold these words, says the First and the Last, who died and lives again.

⁹ For I, (Yeshua) I know your deeds and sorrows, and the blasphemy of those who say they are - "people of Yehovah" (Yehudim) - Jews, but are not. They are the sons of Satan.

¹⁰ Do not fear them (sons of Satan). Behold! Satan will possess them in order to test you. The tribulation

will last for ten days. May you be faithful until the day of your death, so that I may give to you the crown of life.

¹¹ Whoever has ears, let him hear what the Spirit says to the assemblies: Whoever overcomes will not find himself afflicted with the second death.

¹² Write to the messenger of the assembly of Pergamos, he who has the sharp two-edged sword in his hand says these things:

¹³ I know the place where you dwell. You dwell in the place where Satan is enthroned. Yet you still keep my name and you do not deny my faith. In past days, Antipas, my faithful witness, was killed near you, where Satan dwells.

¹⁴ Still, I have matters to bring against you. There are those found among you who follow the teaching of Balaam, who taught Balak to set a trap in the midst of the sons of Israel, to feast (revel) and commit whoredom.

¹⁵ Indeed, there are also found among you those who follow the teaching of the Nicolaitans.

¹⁶ Therefore, repent, and if not, behold I will come in haste and I will fight with them (followers of Balaam & the Nicolaitans) with the sword of my mouth.

¹⁷ Whoever has ears, hear what the Spirit says to the assemblies: Whoever overcomes - I will give to him the hidden manna - and I will give to him a stone to build with my name written upon the stone - a name that no one knows - except he who accepts it.

¹⁸ And to the messenger of the assembly of Thyatira; write these words says the Son of Elohim - Who has eyes like a flame of fire, and feet resembling bronze burning in the furnace.

¹⁹ I know your works, and your faith and your love. Also, I know your intimacy (with God), and your service, and your latter works which are greater than the former.

²⁰ Nonetheless, I have a few things against you, because you allow to remain that woman Jezebel. She

says she is a prophetess, but teaches falsely, misleading my servants to commit fornication, and eat of sacrifices to idols.

²¹ I gave her (Jezebel) time to return in repentance, but she did not want to return from her fornication.

²² Behold, I banish her to a time of mourning, and those who commit fornication with her. They will be in great trouble if they do not repent regarding their deeds.

²³ And her sons will die with death. All the assemblies will know that I search hearts and minds. I will give to each and every one of you according to your deeds.

²⁴ I say to you, the others who are in Thyatira, who do not have the knowledge (to interpret prophecy) - and who do not know the depths of Satan - I will not send you another oracle.

²⁵ But what you have now - hold on to - hold on until I come.

²⁶ And to him (Yeshua) who overcomes and stands fast until the end, I will give dominion over the nations.

²⁷ (Yeshua) will triumph over them (the nations) with a scepter of iron - they will be as earthen vessels smashed like a battering-ram.

²⁸ As I received it from my Father - "I will give to Him the morning star."

²⁹ Whoever has ears, hear what the Spirit says to the assemblies.

Chapter 3

¹ To the messenger of the church in Sardis write; These things, says

he (Yeshua) who has the seven Spirits of (Yehovah), and the seven Stars; I know your works - because you have a name that you are alive - but behold you are dying.

² You must work diligently and stay strong about the things within you which are yet to die: For I have found

that your mission before Yehovah is not yet finished.

³ You yourself will remember when you took hold of the Shema, observed it, and made Teshuvah (repent and return to Yehovah): If you do not watch diligently, I (Yeshua) will come upon you like a thief (in the night), and you will not know the hour in which I will come.

⁴ However, there are a few in Sardis who have not defiled their garments; and they shall walk with me (Yeshua) in white garments, because they are worthy.

⁵ He who overcomes - he shall therefore be clothed in white raiment. Neither will I blot out his name from the book of life - instead - I (Yeshua) will praise his name before my Father, and before His angels.

⁶ He who has ears, let him hear what the Spirit will say unto the assemblies.

⁷ To the messenger of the church of Philadelphia write, behold the things I say - who is holy and true - and has the key of David which opens what no one can shut thereafter, and closes what no one can open thereafter.

⁸ I know your works: Behold! I have set before you an open portal, which no one will be able to shut by any means. You have little strength, yet you have kept my Word, and you have not denied my name (Yeshua).

⁹ I (Yeshua) will give notice to the assembly of Satan, those which say they are Yehudim (People of Yehovah), but are not, because they are liars! Behold I (Yeshua) will make them come in supplication - and they will bow at Your (Yehovah's) feet - and know that I (Yeshua) myself have loved You!

¹⁰ Since you have kept the gift of my word, therefore, I will keep you from the hour of temptation, which will come upon all the inhabitants of the land - to test all those who dwell in the earth.

¹¹ Behold, I (Yeshua) will come swiftly, in haste. Guard what you have (my Word) - so that no one will take your crown.

¹² He who overcomes, I will raise him up to stand in

the temple of my God. He will go out no more. Also, I will write upon him the name of my Elohim and the name of the city of my Elohim - the New Jerusalem - which is descended from the heavens from my Elohim with my name.

¹³ Whoever has ears (to hear the truth), let him hear what the Spirit will say to the assemblies.

¹⁴ And to the messenger of the assembly of Laodiceans, write these words said the Amen, the faithful and true witness, who is the first creation of Elohim.

¹⁵ I know your deeds, that you are neither hot nor cold: O that you were either hot or, at least, cold!

¹⁶ But since you are lukewarm, I will start to vomit you out.

¹⁷ Since you say "I am wealthy and made rich and do not need anything."

Behold you do not know that you are poor and blind and naked!

¹⁸ I counsel you to buy from me refined gold, so that you too will be refined, in order that you will be abundant, clothed in white clothing so that the nakedness of your stupidity will not be seen. And you will anoint your eyes so that you will see.

¹⁹ Since I, myself correct and chastise those that I love, in the same way be zealous and return in repentance unto me like this.

²⁰ Behold! I stand at the door knocking, and if he who will hear my voice, will open the door for me, I will come in unto him and eat the evening meal with him, and he with me.

²¹ He who overcomes I will grant dominion to sit with me at my throne, even as I also overcame and sat with my Father at His throne.

²² He who has ears (to hear the truth), let him hear what the Spirit will say unto the assemblies.

Chapter 4

¹ After these things, I looked, and behold there was a portal open in the heavens. The first voice I heard was as the sound of the shofar speaking with me, saying, "Come up, I implore you, and behold, I will show you what must happen soon."

² After these things I was in the Spirit, and behold, a throne was placed in the heavens, and the One who sits on the throne appeared.

³ The one who sits on it (the throne), His face resembles a precious stone, such as jasper or ruby. And a rainbow around the throne resembles an emerald.

⁴ And around that throne were placed twenty-four seats, and upon the seats sat twenty-four elders clothed in white raiment, and upon their heads, crowns of gold.

⁵ And from the throne went forth lightning and thunder and flashes of fire.

Seven burning lamps were before the throne, which are the seven Spirits of Elohim.

⁶ And before the throne, it was as a sea of glass, like unto crystal. In the midst of the throne, and around the throne, were four living creatures filled with eyes in front and back.

⁷ And the first living creature resembled a lion. And the second living creature resembled a young bullock. And the third living creature resembled the face of a man. And the fourth living creature resembled an eagle in flight.

⁸ Each and every one of the four living creatures has six wings roundabout, and are filled with eyes, and they will not rest day or night saying, "Holy! Holy! Holy! Elohim the Almighty who was, and is, and Who will be!"

⁹ These same living creatures gave honor and blessing to Him who sits on the throne, who lives forever and ever.

¹⁰ Behold, the twenty-four elders fell prostrate before the One who sits on the throne. They worshiped Him who lives forever and ever. They put the crowns from their heads before the throne, saying:

¹¹ "I beseech You, Yehovah our Elohim, You are worthy to bring the glory and the majesty and the might, as You have made all things, which by Your will they exist and were created."

Chapter 5

¹ I saw, in the right hand of the One (Yehovah) sitting upon the throne, a book written front and back, sealed with seven seals.

² I saw a powerful angel calling out with a great voice, "Who, I pray you, is worthy to open the book and to break the seals?"

³ None was found that could open the book, detach its seals, and look at it - not in the heavens, nor on earth, nor under the earth.

⁴ I wept bitterly because no one was found worthy to open the book and to look in it.

⁵ One of the elders said to me, "Do not weep! Behold! The Lion of the tribe of Judah (Yeshua) - from the Root of David - overcame to open the book and to remove the seven seals.

⁶ And behold, I saw - in the midst of the throne and the four living creatures, and in the midst of the twenty four elders - a lamb standing, which had been slain - who had seven horns and seven eyes that are the seven spirits of Elohim, which are sent over all the earth.

⁷ He came and he took the book from the right hand of the One sitting upon the throne.

⁸ After that he (Yeshua) opened the book: Behold! The four divine living creatures and the twenty four elders prostrated themselves before the Lamb! In the

hand of each and every one are stringed instruments and bowls made of gold, full of sweet incense - which are the prayers of the holy ones.

⁹ They sang a new song, saying, "You, Adonai, are worthy to take the book and to unlock the seals - because you were slain - our salvation, our deliverance is by your blood - for every tribe and tongue, for every people, and for every nation."

¹⁰ You made us a kingdom of priests for our Elohim, and we will reign over the earth.

¹¹ I saw and I heard the sound of many angels around the throne and divine living creatures and elders, and their number was thousands of thousands.

¹² They proclaimed with a loud voice to the lamb who was slain - you are worthy to receive power, divinity, strength, glory, and honor and blessing.

¹³ From all creation which is in heaven and in earth, and under the earth, and who are in the sea, and in the midst of it - I heard all of them saying to Him Who sits on the throne and to the Lamb, "The blessing and glory and honor and dominion be forever and ever."

¹⁴ The four divine living creatures said, "Amen!" And the twenty-four elders fell upon their faces and worshiped the One Who lives forever and ever.

Chapter 6

¹ When I saw that the Lamb had opened the first seal from the seven seals, I then heard one of the four divine living creatures, who said in a thunderous voice, "Come and see!"

² I saw and beheld a white horse. He who sat upon it has a bow in his right hand. He was given a crown, and he went out so as to conquer, that he may overcome.

³ After he opened the second seal, I heard the second divine living creature saying, "Come and see!"

⁴ Another horse went forth that was red. And he who sat upon it was given authority to take peace from the land, that a man would be able to put his neighbor to a violent death. A great sword was given to him.

⁵ When he (the Lamb - Yeshua) opened the third seal, I heard the third creature, who said, "Come and see!" And behold! - a black horse, and he who sat upon it had scales in his hand.

⁶ And I heard a voice, in the midst of the four creatures, saying, "Behold! - two measures of wheat kernels in exchange for one small coin, and six measures of barley in exchange for one small coin. But do not forget to preserve the wine and the oil."

⁷ When he (Yeshua) opened the fourth seal, I heard the voice of the fourth creature, saying, "Come and see!"

⁸ Behold! - a dappled horse, and he who sat upon it was named Death, and She'ol (Hell) followed after him. He was given power over the four corners of the earth - to cause death with the sword, with famine and with pestilence against the living creatures on the earth.

⁹ When he had opened the fifth seal, I saw under the altar the souls of those slain because of the word of Yehovah - and because of their testimony.

¹⁰ They cried out in a great voice saying, "How long, blessed Lord, until you judge and take vengeance for our blood, shed by the hand of those who dwell upon the earth?"

¹¹ They will all be given - each and every one - white garments. It was said to them that they may rest until the time of the harvest, until the number of their friends and brothers that will be martyred shall be fulfilled.

¹² When he opened the sixth seal, I saw a great deafening earthquake. The sun became black like sackcloth made from goats' hair. The whiteness of the moon became as blood!

¹³ The stars fell from the heavens to the earth, like a fig tree casting off its figs when shaken by a great wind.

[14] The heavens were pushed away from their places, like a scroll when rolled up. Every mountain and every island was shaken.

[15] The kings of the earth, the officers, the tribes, the rich, the powerful, and every servant and freeman hid themselves in caves, and commanded the mountains:

[16] Saying to the mountains and the cliffs, "Cause yourselves to fall on us and hide us from the eyes of Him who is dwelling upon the throne, and from the anger of the Lamb,

[17] because the great day of His wrath has come!" But who is able to stand?

Chapter 7

[1] After this I saw four angels standing upon the four corners of the earth, restraining in their hands the four winds of the earth, that they should not blow upon the land or upon the sea or upon any tree.

[2] Afterward I saw a messenger from the angels ascending from the east of the sun - who had the seal of the living El (Elohim). He called out with a great voice to the four angels, which were given authority to destroy the land and the sea.

[3] The (Voice) said, "Do not damage the land nor the sea, nor even a tree, until we have marked a Tav (sign) on the foreheads of the servants of Yehovah."

[4] I heard the number of them who had been marked by Him, and they will be 144,000 from all the tribes of the sons of Israel.

[5] From the tribe of Yehudah (Judah) 12,000 were marked. Of the tribe of Rueben 12,000 were marked. Of the tribe of Gad 12,000 were marked.

[6] From the tribe of Asher 12,000 were marked. Of the tribe of Naphtali 12,000 were marked. From the tribe of Menasheh 12,000 were marked.

[7] From the tribe of Shimon 12,000 were marked. Of

the tribe of Levi 12,000 were marked. From the tribe of Yissaschar 12,000 were marked.

⁸ From the tribe of Zevulun 12,000 were marked. Of the tribe of Yosef 12,000 were marked. Of the tribe of Bin'yamin 12,000 were marked.

⁹ After that I saw a great multitude that could not be numbered from all nations, and families, and people, and tongues standing before the throne - in front of the eyes of the Lamb - clothed in white robes with palm branches in their hands.

¹⁰ They cried out with a great voice, "Salvation to those belonging to Yehovah - who sits upon the throne - and unto the Lamb!"

¹¹ The angels standing around the throne, also the elders, and the four divine living creatures - fell upon their faces, worshiping before the throne of Yehovah.

¹² They said, "So may it be! The blessing, and might, and strength, be unto our Elohim for ever and ever! Amen!

¹³ One of the elders answered and said to me, "Behold, those dressed in white robes - who are these, or rather, where are they from?"

¹⁴ I (John) said unto him, "My lord, excuse me - but you know!" And he said to me, "Behold! These are the ones who came out of great tribulation and have washed and purified their robes - and made them white by the blood of the Lamb."

¹⁵ "For this reason they are before the throne of Yehovah - having been consecrated in His Temple, they are serving Him day and night. He who sits upon the throne will dwell among them."

¹⁶ "They will not hunger nor thirst, nor be afflicted by the scorching heat of the sun."

¹⁷ "For the Lamb will lead them, saying, 'Come to the Water of Life!' Yehovah Elohim will wipe all tears from their eyes."

Chapter 8

[1] When he opened the seventh seal: behold, all became silent in heaven for an hour.

[2] Then I saw seven angels standing before Yehovah, and they were given seven shofars.

[3] Another angel came and he stood before the altar, having a censer of gold; and they gave him much incense to deliver prayers of all the holy ones upon the altar of gold, which is before the throne.

[4] And the smoke from the incense rose up with the prayers of the holy ones, from the hand of the angel who was before Yehovah.

[5] And the angel took the golden censer, and he filled it with the altar's fire, and he threw it to the earth. Then the sounds became a deafening thunder, and lightning,
and an earthquake.

[6] The seven angels with the seven shofars were prepared to sound their shofars.

[7] And the first angel sounded the shofar and there was hail, and fire mixed with blood, and it fell upon the earth. A third of the trees burned, and all the greenery burned.

[8] Then the second angel sounded the shofar, and the great mountain burning with fire fell into the sea, and a third of the sea became as blood.

[9] A third of the creatures which were alive in the sea - died - and a third of the ships were lost.

[10] The third angel sounded the shofar, and there fell from heaven a great star, burning like a torch, and it fell into a third of the rivers and wells of water.

[11] The name of the star was Wormwood, and a third of the water turned scarlet, and many people died from the water because it turned bitter.

[12] Then the fourth angel sounded the shofar - and a third of the sun, the moon, and the stars became eclipsed,

that third would not shine, neither by night nor by day.

[13] And I saw and heard the sound of an angel who hovered in the heavens saying, "Oi, Oi, Oi, to those dwelling upon the earth - because of the clarion calls of the last three angels who have yet to sound their shofars."

Chapter 9

[1] And the fifth angel sounded the shofar, and I saw a star from heaven fall upon the earth. The key to the deep was given to him (the fifth angel).

[2] He opened the pit of the deep, and smoke from the pit rose like smoke from a great furnace, the sun and the air were darkened by the smoke of the pit.

[3] Out of the smoke of the pit - locusts came out upon the earth and they were given dominion, as the scorpions were given dominion on earth.

[4] They were commanded not to destroy the grass of the earth, nor any green plant, nor any tree, but only (to attack) the people who do not have the seal of Yehovah on their foreheads.

[5] No authority was given to them to kill people, but only to grieve them for five months - with the sting of scorpions they would torment mankind.

[6] In those days, men will seek death, but will not find it. They will greatly yearn to die, but death will flee from them.

[7] The locusts resembled warhorses prepared for battle. Upon their heads were a likeness crowned with gold - and their faces were like the faces of men.

[8] Their hair was fine like the hair of women. Their teeth were like the teeth of lions.

[9] They had body armor, resembling iron breastplates, and the sound of their wings was like the sound of chariot horses charging into battle.

[10] They had tails like scorpions. They stung with

their tails those under their power - to torment people for a duration of five months.

[11] They had their king, the angel of the abyss, whose name in Hebrew is Abaddon, and in the Greek tongue, Apollyon, and in the Roman tongue, Terminus.

[12] One woe has passed. Behold! Two more woes are coming!

[13] The sixth angel sounded the shofar, and I heard a voice coming from the light of the golden altar, which is before Yehovah.

[14] (The Voice) said to the sixth angel with the shofar, "Loose the four (fallen) angels which are bound under the great river Euphrates."

[15] The four (fallen) angels were let loose - who had been prepared for the hour, for the day, for the month, and for the year - to kill a third of mankind.

[16] And the number of their army of horsemen was twenty times ten thousand, and I heard their number, 200,000.

[17] And so I saw the vision of the horses, and those who sat on them had body armor of fire, brimstone, and sulfur. The heads of the horses were like the heads of lions. Out of their mouths came fire, smoke, and brimstone.

[18] And by these three plagues, (fire, smoke, brimstone) a third of the sons of mankind were killed.

[19] The power of the horses is in their mouths and in their tails. Their tails are like serpents, with which they kill!

[20] Nonetheless, there were many children of mankind who cannot be put to death by these strikes - because they repented of their evil deeds. They do not pray to Satan nor to idols of clay, stone, wood, silver, or gold - which are not able to walk or speak or hear.

[21] There are still those who did not repent of their murders, nor of their sorceries, nor of their fornications, nor of their thefts. They shall not die a natural death!

Chapter 10

¹ I saw another mighty angel who came down from the heavens, clothed in a cloud, and there was a rainbow upon his head. His face was like the sun, and his feet were like pillars of fire.

² He had an open book in his hand, and put his right foot on the sea, and his left foot on the earth.

³ He called out with a great voice like unto the lion roaring, and as he called out, the seven voices of the lightnings thundered their words.

⁴ After the voices of the seven lightnings spoke their words - I wanted to write - but lo! I heard a divine voice from the heavens say to me, "Seal that which the voices of the seven lightnings spoke, and do not write their words!"

⁵ The angel - which I saw standing on the sea and on the earth - he lifted his hands to the heavens.

⁶ He swore by the Eternal Living One, who created the heavens and all that exists - the earth, the sea, and all that is in them - "There is no more time!"

⁷ Once the seventh angel blows his shofar - all the secrets of Yehovah will be accomplished - just as He revealed by the hand of the prophets, His servants!

⁸ I heard again the divine voice saying to me, "Go and take the open book from the hand of the angel who stands on the sea and the earth."

⁹ So I went to the angel and said to him, "Please give me the book!" And he said to me, "Take the book and swallow it, for it will be like honey in your mouth - but bitter in your bowels."

¹⁰ I took the book from the angel's hand, and I swallowed it, and it was sweet like honey in my mouth - but when I swallowed it, behold, it became bitter in my stomach.

¹¹ Then he said to me, "Behold, You must prophesy again to nations, peoples and to sovereigns."

Chapter 11

[1] There was given me a reed like unto a rod, and it was said to me - Arise and measure the temple of Yehovah and the altar, and those who pray therein.

[2] The courtyard which is outside the temple - do not measure it! For forty-two months (lunar cycles) it has been given to the nations to trample the Holy City.

[3] And I will give my two witnesses to prophesy 1,260 days, wearing sackcloth.

[4] These are the two olive trees, and the two Menorahs, standing before the Elohim of the earth.

[5] If anyone wants to harm these two, behold, fire will come out from their mouths and will devour their enemies - and they will be slain.

[6] They have the power to shut the heavens so that there will be no rain during the days of their prophecy. They also have the power over the waters to turn them into blood, and to smite the earth with all sorts of plagues as they will.

[7] When they have finished their prophecy, behold, the beast will come up from the abyss and make war against them. He will defeat them and kill them.

[8] Their corpses will be thrown into the streets of the Holy City - which is called the spirit of Sodom and Egypt - because there our Lord was crucified.

[9] And the nations will see their corpses for a duration of three and a half days - and they shall no be buried.

[10] Some on the earth will rejoice over them (& their death). They will send gifts one to another because these two prophets brought grief to many residing upon the earth.

[11] After three and a half days the Spirit of Life from Elohim re-entered them. They rose to their feet - and a great terror fell upon certain who saw them!

[12] And they (the two witnesses) heard a great voice

from heaven saying, "Come up here!" And they rose up in a cloud unto heaven, and their enemies saw them.

¹³ In that very hour there was a great earthquake - and a tenth part - the richest part of the city fell. Seven thousand people died - and a great fear fell upon the others - and they gave praise to Elohim in heaven.

¹⁴ The second woe is passed, and the third comes quickly!

¹⁵ Then the seventh angel blew his shofar, and great voices were heard in heaven, singing the music of creation, "The kingdoms of this world have returned to our Lord God by the hand of our Lord Yeshua, and he will reign forever and ever. Amen!"

¹⁶ And the twenty-four elders - who sit before Yehovah - fell upon their faces from their chairs and worshiped Yehovah.

¹⁷ They were saying, "We praise You Yehovah, Lord of Hosts! You are the Almighty - Who is, Who was, and Who will be! - For surely by Your power and might You reign."

¹⁸ The time of the nations is complete. Therefore the time of Your wrath and judgment of the dead has come - to give recompense to your servants, the holy prophets, and the righteous who revere You - and judge the great and the small - and destroy those who corrupted the earth.

¹⁹ The Temple of Yehovah aka (House of prayer) was opened in heaven, and the Ark of the tablets of the Covenant was revealed in His Temple- and coming from it were thunder, lightning and great hailstones.

Chapter 12

¹ A great sign appeared in the heavens; a woman clothed with the sun, and the moon beneath her

² She was with child, crying out - afflicted with birth pains - that she might give birth.

³ And there appeared another sign in heaven - behold, a great fiery dragon, having seven heads and ten horns, and on his heads were seven crowns.

⁴ His tail swept away a third of the stars of heaven and threw them to the earth. The dragon stood before the woman about to give birth - so that when she gave birth - he might devour her child (the body of Christ).

⁵ She gave birth to a male child - who is destined to rule all the nations with a sceptre of iron. Her child was caught up to Yehovah and to His throne.

⁶ The woman fled into the wilderness, where she had a place prepared by Yehovah, so that there she can be nourished for one thousand two hundred and sixty days.

⁷ Then a great war arose in heaven - Michael (the archangel) and his angels fighting against the dragon. And the dragon and his (fallen) angels fought back.

⁸ But they did not prevail, and there was no longer any place for them in heaven.

⁹ That great dragon was thrown down, the ancient serpent, who is called Satan - the deceiver of the whole world - was thrown down to the earth, and his angels were thrown down with him.

¹⁰ I heard a great voice in the heavens that said, "Now we will see salvation and the mighty deeds of our Elohim and His Messiah - because he (Satan) has been cast out who was their adversary - who accuses the brethren day and night before our God."

¹¹ They have conquered him (Satan) by the blood of the Lamb and by the Word of his Covenant - for they loved not their lives even unto death.

¹² Therefore, rejoice O heavens and all who live in them! But woe to those who dwell in the land and the sea - for Satan has come down to you with his great wrath - knowing that his time is short.

¹³ When the dragon saw that he had been banished to the earth - he pursued the woman of Shiloh - who had given birth to the male child (the body of Christ).

¹⁴ The woman was given two wings of a great eagle - so that she might fly into the wilderness - to a place chosen by Yehovah where she will be provided for a time, times, and a half a time, away from the presence of the serpent.

¹⁵ To silence her, the serpent poured water like a great flood out of his mouth - after the woman - to sweep her away.

¹⁶ The woman was delivered by the earth - which opened its mouth and swallowed the waters that the dragon had cast after her.

¹⁷ The dragon became furious with the woman and went to make war with the remnant of her seed - those who keep the commandments of Yehovah and hold to the Covenant of Yeshua the Messiah.

Chapter 13

¹ Then I stood upon the sand of the sea. I saw a beast rising from the sea. It had seven heads and ten horns. Upon its horns were ten crowns. Upon its (seven) heads were blasphemous names of slander and mockery *of God!*

² And the beast that I saw was like a leopard. His feet were like the feet of a bear.

His mouth was like the mouth of a lion. The dragon gave the beast his power and great authority.

³ I saw one of its heads. It had been mortally wounded - but its deadly wound was healed. All the world marveled and followed the beast.

⁴ They worshiped the dragon who gave power to the beast. They also worshiped the beast, saying, "Who is like the beast? Who is able to wage war with him?"

⁵ It was given to it (the beast) to speak boastful words and blasphemies - and it was given power to act for forty-two months.

⁶ She (the beast) opened her mouth in blasphemy

against Yehovah, to blaspheme His Name and His tabernacle, and those who dwell in heaven.

[7] Power was given to the beast to wage war with the saints and to overcome them. It was given power over every tribe and people and tongue and nation.

[8] All the inhabitants of the earth are worshiping the beast. Everyone whose name was not written in the book of life of the Lamb who has been slain - anointed since the foundation of the world.

[9] If anyone has ears - listen and heed!

[10] Whoever has taken a prisoner - he will be taken prisoner. Likewise, he who kills by the sword - he will be killed by the sword. However, with the saints - there is hope and faith!

[11] Then I saw another creature coming up out of the earth - and it had two horns like a lamb - and it spoke like a serpent.

[12] It exercised all of the power of the first beast - and it caused all the earth and its inhabitants to worship the first beast - which was healed from the deadly wound.

[13] It will perform great signs, even making fire come down from heaven onto the earth in the sight of men.

[14] It deceived the inhabitants of the earth by the performance of signs and wonders - that were permitted to be done by the beast - saying to the inhabitants of the earth - make an image of the beast mortally wounded by a sword who yet lived.

[15] It was given power to give breath to the image of the beast - that the image of the beast will speak and cause those to be killed - who would not worship the image of the beast.

[16] It will force everyone - the small and great, the rich and poor, the children of the free and the slaves - to receive a mark upon their hand, or forehead.

[17] So that no one may buy or sell - except the one who has the mark of the beast - or the number of his name.

[18] Here is wisdom and understanding. Let one who is mindful calculate the number of the beast - for it is the number belonging to one man (Adam): His number is 666.

Chapter 14

¹ I looked and behold! A Lamb (Yeshua) stood upon Mount Zion, and with him 144,000 upon whose foreheads is written the name of his Father (Yehovah).

² I heard a voice from heaven - like the voice of many waters - and like the sound of a great earthquake. The sound that I heard was much like the music of the stringed instruments which they were playing.

³ They sang a renewed song before the throne, and before the four divine living beings, and the elders, and certainly no one was able to learn the song, except the 144,000 who were purchased from the earth (with the blood of Yeshua).

⁴ These are those who were with women - but they were not defiled - because they are still as virgins. These follow after the Lamb everywhere that he goes. They are people who have been redeemed for Yehovah - and for the lamb - they are the firstfruits.

⁵ In their mouths deception was not found, because they were blameless before the throne of

⁶ I saw another angel flying in the midst of heaven - bringing the everlasting good news to declare to those who dwell upon the earth - for all the nations, tribes, tongues, and peoples.

⁷ Saying to them in a great voice: "Fear Elohim, and give him glory, because the hour of His judgment has come. And they worshiped Him Who made the heavens, and the earth, and the seas, and the springs.

⁸ Another angel followed, saying, "She is fallen! She is fallen! Babylon the great - who made the whole earth delirious from her wine - which the nations drank - causing madness to fall upon the nations!"

⁹ The third angel followed after them, saying in a great voice (that) if anyone worship the beast, and his

image, and takes the mark in his forehead, or in his hand -

[10] - they will drink from the wine of the fierce wrath of Elohim, which is mixed in the cup of his wrath. He will mix it with troubles, fire, and brimstone, in the presence of the Lamb and his holy angels.

[11] The smoke of their torment will rise forever and ever - not one of them will have rest day or night, who worshiped the beast and its image - whoever took the mark of its name.

[12] Here is found what the saints were waiting for - those who keep the commandments of Yehovah - and the faith of Yeshua.

[13] I heard a divine voice from the heavens say to me, "Write! - blessed are those who die for the holiness of Yehovah - for the Spirit says those who live by their deeds - their deeds will follow them."

[14] I looked and behold! There was a white cloud - upon the cloud someone sits like the Son of man - who has a golden crown upon his head - and a sharp sickle in his hand.

[15] Another angel came out of the temple - calling in a divine voice to he who sat on the cloud, "Send forth, please your sickle and reap - because the hour has come to reap - the harvest of the earth is ripe."

[16] He who was sitting on the cloud sent forth his sickle to the earth - and the earth was reaped.

[17] Another angel appeared from the temple which was in heaven. He also had a sharp sickle.

[18] Yet another angel went out from the altar and he had authority over fire. With the sickle in his hand, he shouted with a loud voice, "Strike with your sickle and harvest the grapes of the earth, because her fruits have ripened!"

[19] The angel struck with his sickle and harvested the grapes of the earth and threw them in the great winepress of the wrath of Yehovah.

[20] The winepress was trodden outside the city - and

blood came out from the winepress up to the horses' bridles for a length of some 1600 furlongs.

Chapter 15

[1] I saw another sign in heaven, great and astonishing! Seven angels were coming and in their hands were the seven last plagues - the final wrath of Elohim - yet to be fulfilled!

[2] I saw a vision, like unto a sea of crystal glass mixed with fire. They who overcame the beast and its idol - and the number of its name - were standing on the sea of crystal glass - holding the harps of Elohim -

[3] And (they were) singing the song of Moses, servant of Elohim - and the song of the Lamb, saying - "Great and marvelous are Your works - Yehovah, God of Hosts - Righteous and true are your ways, Oh King of kings!"

[4] " Who will not fear you, nor magnify Your Name, oh Elohim? Truly, You alone are righteous - all the nations will come and bow down before you - as your judgments are revealed!

[5] After this - Behold! I saw the ark of the covenant was opened in the heavens.

[6] Seven angels appeared from the temple - who had the seven plagues - clothed in pure bright linen - their chests girded with golden belts.

[7] One of the four divine living creatures gave unto the seven angels - seven golden bowls - full of the wrath of Yehovah - Who lives forever and ever.

[8] The temple of God (house of prayer) was filled with the glory of Yehovah and His mighty power - no one will be able to enter the temple until the seven plagues of the seven angels are fulfilled!

Chapter 16

[1] I heard the great voice from heaven proclaiming to the seven angels, "Go, and pour out the seven cups of Yehovah's wrath on the earth!"

[2] The first angel went and poured out his bowl upon the earth - and a heavy plague came upon the earth. It was very, very bad for the people who had the mark of the beast on them - who prostrated themselves before the beast and its image.

[3] The second angel poured out his bowl into the sea - and it was changed into the blood of the dying - and every living creature which it touched died in the sea.

[4] The third (angel) poured out his bowl into rivers and reservoirs of water, and the waters became blood.

[5] I heard the angel of the waters saying, "You, Yehovah, the Righteous One - Who was, Who is and Who will be - are holy and You have judged this. "

[6] Since they have shed the blood of saints and prophets - You have given them(deadly) blood to drink- for they deserve it!

[7] Then I heard a second (voice) saying, "Truly! Yehovah, God Almighty - Your judgments are righteous and true."

[8] The fourth angel poured out his bowl into the sun - giving it power to afflict the world with great fire and destruction!

[9] They (the unrepentant ones) blasphemed the name of Yehovah - Who has authority over these plagues and they did not return in repentance to give Him glory.

[10] The fifth angel poured out his bowl upon the throne of the beast; and its kingdom became darkness. They gnawed their tongues from anguish and pain.

[11] They cursed the God of the heavens because of their pain and wounds - but they did not turn back in repentance of their deeds.

[12] The sixth angel poured out his bowl into that great River Euphrates and dried up its waters to prepare the way for the kings from the east (sunrise).

[13] I saw, coming out from the mouth of the dragon, and from the mouth of the beast, and from the mouth of the prophet of deceit, three unclean spirits resembling reptiles!

[14] They (the reptiles) are the spirits of demons, performing signs, and going out to the kings of all the earth to gather them for the war of the great day against God Almighty.

[15] Behold, I come stealthily. Blessed is he who is vigilant and maintains his garments (armor) - who does not walk uncovered so they will not see his shame.

[16] He (Yehovah) will gather them in a place called (in Hebrew) "Armageddon."

[17] Then the seventh angel poured out his bowl upon the wind - and there came a great voice out of the temple, from the throne, saying, "It is finished!"

[18] And there was great lightning and sounds of thunder - and huge earthquakes like have never happened since there were humans on the earth.

[19] The great city was split into three parts. The cities of the nations fell. Babylon the Great was judged before God to give unto her the bowl of His fierce wrath.

[20] Islands disappeared - and mountains (were levelled) - could no longer be found.

[21] Huge hailstones the weight of a talent came down from heaven upon mankind. People cursed God because the death from the hailstones was very great!

Chapter 17

[1] There came one of the seven angels - who had one of the seven bowls - came and spoke with me, saying, "Come and I will show you the judgment of the great harlot who sits upon the many waters.

2 With her the kings of the earth have fornicated, and the inhabitants of the earth have become drunk with the wine of her fornication!"

3 The hand of the Spirit brought me into the wilderness. I saw her - the one who sits on the scarlet beast - full of the reproach of her blasphemous names, having seven heads and ten horns.

4 The woman was dressed in scarlet and blue, and decked out with gold, precious stones, and pearls - having a golden cup in her hand full of abomination - full of the uncleanness of her fornication rites.

5 On her forehead was written the name - Mystery Babylon the Great - the mother of harlots and abominations of the earth.

6 And I saw a woman drunk from the blood of the saints - the blood of the martyrs for Yeshua! I was completely astonished at what I saw!

7 The angel said to me, Why are you so astonished? Behold, I will tell you the secret of the woman - and the beast which is carrying her - having seven heads and ten horns.

8 Behold, the beast which you saw - was and is no more - and will come up from the abyss and go to Sheol. The inhabitants of the earth will be shocked - those whose names are not written in the Book of Life - from the beginning of the world - they see the beast that was and is no more.

9 "This is the meaning of wisdom. The seven heads, they are the seven mountains upon which the woman dwells - and which are the seven (fallen) angels."

10 Also seven kings, five of them are fallen, and one still is and the other has not yet come. When he comes his time will be short.

11 The beast - which was, but is not - is the eighth (fallen angel), and is with the seven who go down to defeat and Sheol.

12 The ten horns that you saw - they are ten kings

which have not yet received a kingdom - but they received power as kings for one hour to rule along with the beast.

¹³ To these (kings) was given one purpose - their forces shall be given to the beast.

¹⁴ They will make war with the Lamb - and the Lamb will prevail over them! For he is the Lord of Lords, and King of kings - and those with him are his chosen believers.

¹⁵ And he said to me, "The waters which you saw there - where the harlot sits -

they are the multitudes, and nations, and tongues.

¹⁶ The ten horns that you saw on the beast (the ten kings), they are haters of the whore - and they

¹⁷ Because God has given into their hearts that they will accomplish His will - and they will give the kingdom to the beast - until they fulfill the word of Elohim.

¹⁸ The woman which you saw - she is the great city - which rules over all the kings of the earth.

Chapter 18

¹ After these things I saw another angel coming down from heaven with great power, and great courage, and the earth was lit by his splendor.

² He proclaimed strongly, saying, "Fallen! Fallen! - is Babylon the great! And she has become a dwelling place of demons, along with every unclean spirit, guarded by vultures.

³ All nations have drunk from the wine of her fornication! The kings of the earth have committed fornication with her - and by her power - merchants of the earth who lusted after her have become rich through her favors.

⁴ I heard another divine voice from heaven saying, "Depart from her! - So that you will not be partakers of her sins and receivers of her plagues."

[5] For her sins have reached unto heaven - and Elohim has judged her iniquities.

[6] Give to her as she gave to you - double doubled according to her evil deeds - and in the cup she poured for you - you shall pour double for her.

[7] How she has glorified herself - and indulged herself! She has made her sins - cause your suffering. Rightly you will give her sorrow - to lament, and mourn - because she said in her heart - I will sit as queen - and I will never be a widow nor know lamentation.

[8] Therefore in one day troubles, death, mourning, and famine will come to her - and she will be burnt by fire - because Elohim, who judges her - is Almighty!

[9] The kings of the earth wept and mourned over her - those who committed fornication with her and lived in self-indulgence - when they saw the smoke of her eternal burning!

[10] They are standing afar - from fear of her torments - saying "Alas, Alas, for the great city Babylon - the mighty city - in one hour your judgment has come!"

[11] The merchants of the earth will weep and mourn for her - because no one will buy anymore:

[12] the purchase of gold, and silver, and precious stones, and pearls, and fine linen, and purple and scarlet silk garments, and all manner of precious woods, and all vessels of ivory, and all jewelry of precious stones, and things of brass, and iron, and marble...

[13] and cinnamon and sweet perfumes, and ointments, and frankincense, and wine, and oil, and sifted fine flour, and wheat, and animals, and sheep, and horses, and chariots, and slaves, and the souls of men.

[14] The fruit of the lust of your soul has come to an end, and all fat and precious things, they are lost from you and they can no longer be found.

[15] The merchants of these goods - which had made them rich - stood afar off from the fear of her torments - weeping, and mourning...

¹⁶ saying, "Woe, woe! To the city that was clothed in fine linen of crimson and blue - and was covered with gold and precious stones and pearls!"

¹⁷ How many riches have been forsaken and lost in one hour! Every ruler, and every passing boat, and all ships and sailors of the sea - stood afar off!

¹⁸ Crying out when they saw the city burning, saying of her, "What city has likened itself to this great city?"

¹⁹ They threw dust upon their heads, and they cried out, weeping and mourning, saying, "Woe, woe to her, the Great City - where they had enriched themselves from their trading - all of them who had ships in the sea - because she was destroyed in one hour!"

²⁰ They exhorted one another over her - the saints and prophets - and rejoiced because Elohim had vindicated their judgments against her.

²¹ An angel took a great stone, like a millstone, and threw it into the sea, saying, "With this mighty tempest you will cast out Babylon the great city - you will no longer find her."

²² The sound of musicians, and singers and pipers, and those lifting the shofar, will no longer be heard in you at all - nor any craftsman or artist be found in you anymore' nor the grinding of a millstone (making flour) shall be heard anymore.

²³ The light of the candle will no longer shine in you, and you will no longer hear the voice of the bridegroom in you - because your merchants were the great powers of the earth - and with your sorceries you misled all the nations.

²⁴ In her was found the blood of the prophets, and the saints, and everyone who was murdered upon the earth.

Chapter 19

¹ After that I heard a voice like that of many trumpets in heaven saying, "Hallelujah! Glory and majesty and

might be to Yehovah!"

² His judgments are true and just - which He (Yehovah) judged against the whore (of Babylon) whose harlotry corrupted all the earth - and He took vengeance upon her who has on her hands the blood of His servants.

³ They said once more: "HalleluYah!" - And the smoke rose up for ever and ever.

⁴ So the twenty-four elders and the four divine living creatures fell down and they worshiped Yehovah who sat upon the throne, saying "Hallelujah! Amen."

⁵ A voice went out from the throne, and said, "Praise Yah, my servants! Praise Yehovah! Praise the name of Yehovah!" - And all the small and great before Him, feared his wrath!"

⁶ I heard the sound of a large multitude - like the sound of many waters - it was like many voices saying, "HalleluYah Yehovah! For the Lord our God, the Almighty is king!"

⁷ "Rejoice and be glad - and give him honor - for the time of the wedding of the Lamb has come and his bride has prepared herself."

⁸ And she (the bride) was given to clothe herself in pure white silk - because it proclaims the righteousness of the saints - and she becomes beautiful.

⁹ He (the angel) said to me - it is written, "Blessed are those who are called to the marriage supper of the Lamb." - "Truly these are the words of Elohim!"

¹⁰ I fell at his feet to bow down to him, and he said to me, "Do not bow down to me - for I serve together with you and the faithful - their testimony of Yeshua came from Yehovah - because the testimony of Yeshua is the spirit of prophecy."

¹¹ I saw the heavens open, and beheld a white horse - and he who sat on it was called Faithful and True. He will conquer and judge in righteousness.

¹² His eyes are like a flame of fire - and on his head are many crowns - and he has a name written which he alone knows.

¹³ His clothing will be stained with blood - His name will be called the Word of God.

¹⁴ All the hosts of heaven, clothed in pure white silk, follow him on white horses.

¹⁵ From his mouth came a two-edged sword to smite the nations - he will reign over them with a sceptre of iron. He treads the winepress of the wrath of Yehovah - Almighty God.

¹⁶ And a name is written upon His clothing, "King of Kings, and Lord of Lords."

¹⁷ I saw an angel standing in the sun - calling with a loud voice - saying to all the carrion birds that fly in the heavens, "Come and gather for the great supper of God!"

¹⁸ And you (vultures) shall eat the flesh of kings - and the flesh of princes - and the flesh of mighty men of war - and the flesh of horses - and the flesh of those who ride on them - and the flesh of the sons of nobles - both the great and the small.

¹⁹ I saw the beast and the kings of the earth and their armies gathered to make war with him (Yeshua) who sat on the white horse - and to fight with his army.

²⁰ The beast and the false prophet were captured while performing miraculous signs - in order to incite those who took the mark of the beast. Those worshiping him (the beast) are then cast alive into Sheol - the lake of fire burning with brimstone.

²¹ The rest were killed by the sword of the Word of God - that comes out of his mouth - who sits on the white horse - and all the beasts of the field feasted upon their flesh.

Chapter 20

¹ I saw an angel coming down from heaven - having the key to the abyss in his hand - and a great chain.

² And he (the angel) took hold of the dragon - the serpent of ancient times - who is the adversary (Satan) and bound him for a thousand years.

³ He sent Satan into the abyss to be imprisoned - and (the angel) sealed it over him (Satan) so that he will no longer deceive the nations - until a thousand years have been completed - after which he will be released for a time.

⁴ I saw thrones, and those sitting upon them who were authorized to judge - those testifying of Yeshua and the Word of God. These are the ones who were slain - who did not take the mark of the beast upon their foreheads or their hands - nor did they worship the beast or his idol. They will live and rule the people with Yeshua for a thousand years.

⁵ However, the rest of the dead do not arise until the thousand years are completed. This is the first resurrection.

⁶ Blessed is he who was set-apart by the first resurrection - for these there will be no second death - Only they shall be priests of Elohim and his Messiah - reigning with them for a thousand years.

⁷ After a thousand years the adversary (Satan) will be released from his prison.

⁸ And he (Satan) shall go and entice the peoples throughout the four corners of the earth, and Gog and Magog, to gather his army for battle - for their number is as the sand of the sea.

⁹ And they went up over the breadth of the earth, and encircled the tents of the saints, and the beloved holy city was filled with fire - and the fire of God came down from heaven and engulfed them (the army of Satan)!

¹⁰ Satan will be cast into the lake of fire and brimstone - where along with the beast and the false prophet they will suffer -day and night - for ever and ever!

¹¹ Then I saw a great, bright throne, and the One sitting on it was He from whom the entities of the earth and the heavens fled - and they found no place for themselves.

¹² I saw the dead, both the least and great, standing before Elohim - and books were opened. Yet another book was opened - this book was the Book of Life - to

judge the dead according to that which was written in the books - according to their deeds.

¹³ Then the sea gave up the dead that were in it. Sheol also gave up its dead who were in it -

¹⁴ Then Death and Gehinnom (Hell itself) will be thrown into the fire: for this is the second death.

¹⁵ Whoever is not found written in the Book of Life - will be thrown into the fire.

Chapter 21

¹ I saw a new heaven and a new earth because the first heaven and the first earth have passed away and the sea is no more.

² Then I, John (Yohanan), saw the city of the Holy One, New Jerusalem, descending from God in heaven - having been made ready as a bride adorned for her husband.

³ I heard a great voice from the throne saying, "Behold, the Tabernacle of Yehovah is among men - and He will dwell with them - and He shall be their God - and they shall be His people.

⁴ Then Yehovah Elohim wiped away the tears from their faces - and there shall be no more death - nor mourning, nor crying, nor pain - there shall be no more - as the former things have passed away.

⁵ And now, he who sits upon the throne says, "Behold, I make everything new!" - and He said to me "Write - for these words are very, very faithful and true!"

⁶ He said to me, "It is finished. I am the Aleph and the Tav - the First and the Last -

the Beginning and the End - I will freely give living water to those who thirst.

⁷ He who prevails will inherit everything. I will be Elohim to him and he will be a son to me.

⁸ However, to the unbelievers, the murderers, the

163

adulterers, the sorcerers, the deceivers - and to all the wicked - I will give a wage of fire from Sheol - the lake which burns by fire and brimstone. This is the second death!

⁹ One of the seven angels came to me - who had in their hands - the bowls which were filled with the seven last plagues - came to me and said, "Come and see the woman, the bride of the Lamb!"

¹⁰ And he carried me in the spirit to a great and lofty mountain and showed me the holy city of Jerusalem coming down from God in heaven.

¹¹ The glory of Yehovah was upon her - and His light was like that of a precious stone called emerald - which is clear as crystal.

¹² It (the holy city) shall have a great and high wall - which shall have twelve gates, and at the gates twelve angels - and written names - which shall be the names of the twelve tribes of the children of Israel.

¹³ From the east three gates and from the north three gates and from the south (Yemen) three gates and from the west three gates.

¹⁴ The wall of the city had twelve foundations - and in them were the names of the twelve sent ones of the Lamb.

¹⁵ He that spoke with me had in his hand a golden reed to measure the city and its gates and wall.

¹⁶ The city shall be square, and its length shall be like a square, and the city shall be measured with the golden reed - and the length and height and width shall be equal.

¹⁷ Its wall measured one hundred and forty-four cubits according to man's measure and that of the angel.

¹⁸ And the building of its wall was of jasper stone, but the city will be pure gold.

¹⁹ The foundation of the wall and the city were adorned with fine stones - the first foundation

²⁰ - The fifth (foundation) was of ruby, the sixth of onyx, the seventh of chrysolite, the eighth of beryl, the ninth of topaz, the tenth of agate, the eleventh of jacinth (or ligure), and the twelfth was called - in a foreign tongue - amethyst.

²¹ The twelve gates shall be twelve pearls - each and every one are pearls - The streets of the city shall be pure gold like clear crystal.

²² I saw no Temple in it - because Yehovah God Almighty and the Lamb - will be His Temple.

²³ And the city needs no light from the sun or moon - because the glory of God and the Lamb will shine upon it.

²⁴ For the blessed ones will walk in the light thereof - and the kings of the earth will bring their wealth into it.

²⁵ The gates will not be closed - because there will be no night there.

²⁶ And they (of the holy city) will bring greatness and splendor to all the nations.

²⁷ And there shall not come in it anything that is defiled or that commits an abomination or deceit - only those written in the Book of Life.

Chapter 22

¹ The angel showed me the river of living water - pure as amethyst - going forth from the throne of God and the Lamb (in the holy city).

² In the midst of its way, here and there, by the river (of living water) will be the tree
of life that yields twelve types of fruit - each for its month. Its fruit is for food - and its leaves are medicine for the healing of the nations.

³ The cursing and destruction will be no more! The throne of Elohim and of the Lamb will be there (in the holy city) and His servants will serve Him.

⁵ There will be no night - neither will they need the light of the sun or moon - for Yehovah will enlighten them - and they will reign (beside Him) forever and ever!

⁶ Then the angel said to me, "These words are absolutely faithful and true - and Yehovah - the God of the spirits

of the prophets - sent His angel to show His servants that which must be done quickly."

[7] "Behold! I (Yeshua) come quickly - blessed is the one who keeps the words of the prophecy of this book."

[8] And I, (John) Yohanan, heard and saw these things - and after I saw and heard - I fell down to bow at his feet (the angel) who showed me these things.

[9] And the angel said to me, "Do not do this! I too serve with you, and your brothers - the prophets - and those who keep the words of this prophecy. Pray to Yehovah!"

[10] The angel said to me, "Do not seal the prophetic vision of this book - because the time is near!"

[11] Whoever is wicked shall be so for all time. Certainly, whoever is impure, will also be the same for all time. However, whoever is righteous will be so for all the time. And whoever is blessed shall continue to be so."

[12] Behold! I come quickly and my reward is with me - to give to each and every one according to their deeds!

[13] I am the Alef and the Tav - the First and the Last - the Beginning and the End!

[14] Blessed are they who have washed their garments in the blood of the Lamb - They shall have the right to eat of the Tree of Life - They shall enter the gates of the holy city.

[15] Those outside - they are dogs, sorcerers, wicked ones, murderers, idolaters, prostitutes and liars.

[16] I, Yeshua, sent my angel to testify to you these things in the assemblies - for I am the root and seed of David - the bright morning star.

[17] For the Spirit and the bride say, "Please come, and he who hears will say come,

[18] I (the angel) testify to all who hear the words of the prophecy of this book: "If anyone adds certain words to it! Elohim will also add to him the plagues written in this book."

[19] If anyone belittles the words of God's prophecy - Elohim will remove his name and inheritance from the book of life - and the holy city - and the blessings written in this book.

[20] He who testifies to these things also said, "I (Yeshua) will come quickly!" Amen! come, Lord Yeshua.

[21] The grace of our Lord Yeshua, the Messiah, be with you all, Amen!"